BIBLE ANSWERS *for* PARENTS *of* Curious Kids

///////////////////////

101 Kid-Friendly Q&As

BARBOUR BOOKS
An Imprint of Barbour Publishing, Inc.

WELCOME TO
BIBLE ANSWERS FOR PARENTS OF CURIOUS KIDS.

If you have children aged five to eight, you know only too well the questions they can come up with. You yourself may not have thought a particular issue through, and may not know how to answer. Rather than giving them a deer-in-the-headlights stare, or winging it, or saying, "Ask your father/mother," you can now give them solid, scriptural answers.

Jesus said, "Love the Lord your God with all your heart, soul and mind" (Matthew 22:37 ICB). Younger children love God with their hearts and souls, so they trust the early, simple explanations. But when they grow older, they require intellectually-satisfying answers if they are to love God with their minds also.

The good news is that God's Word makes sense whatever their age. As the apostle Paul told a Roman governor, "What I am saying is true *and* reasonable" (Acts 26:25 NIV, emphasis added). The Bible is not only true, but it makes logical sense. It's our prayer that you will personally benefit from this book and be excited to share the Q&As with your children. And may the questions that follow each reading spark good parent-child discussions.

1. WHO IS GOD?

\\\\\\\\\\\\\\\\\\\\\\\

God is the great, loving Spirit who lives in heaven. Jesus said many times that God is your "Father in heaven" or "your heavenly Father" (Matthew 5:16, 48; 6:9, 26). So this really is how you should think of Him.

Your heavenly Father is even better than your earthly father. Your Father in heaven always watches over you. He loves you more than you can imagine. He is very kind. Even when bad things happen, He makes sure that everything works out for good in the end.

Think of earthly fathers. They work to earn money so their kids can eat healthy food, wear nice clothes, and have a safe place to live. They provide for them. Jesus said, "Look at the birds... your Father in heaven takes care of them! Aren't you worth much more than birds?" (Matthew 6:26 GNT). Yes, you are! Jesus told you to pray, "Our Father in heaven. . . . Give us today the food we need" (Matthew 6:9, 11 GNT). God wants you to trust that He will give you what you need.

Fathers on earth give their kids gifts, and God does too. Jesus said to Jewish fathers, "If you, then . . .know how to give good gifts to your children, how much more will your Father in heaven give good gifts to those who ask him!" (Matthew 7:11 NIV). God loves you far more than your earthly father and gives you even better gifts.

God also cares for you and protects you. One way He does this is by giving you rules to keep you happy, healthy, and safe. Jesus said, "Those who accept my commandments and obey them are the ones who love me. My Father will love those who love me" (John 14:21 GNT).

God also disciplines you, just like a father. The Bible says, "For the LORD disciplines those he loves. . . . As you endure this divine discipline, remember that God is treating you as his own children. Who ever heard of a child who is never disciplined by its father?" (Hebrews 12:6–7 NLT).

When you disobey God, you make Him sad. But don't worry that He no longer loves you. When children disobey their earthly dad, he might send them to their rooms. But he doesn't kick them out of the house. God is even better! He says, "I will never leave you; I will never abandon you" (Hebrews 13:5 GNT).

God loves you and is always looking out for you!

Can you think of times when God took care of you like a father?

In what other ways is God a Father to you?

2. HOW BIG IS GOD?

\\\\\\\\\\\\\\\\\\\\\\\\\

To understand that question, we need to first of all understand how big the heavens are—because that's where God lives. When we say "the heavens," we usually mean the universe made up of stars and planets and empty space. And it has no end.

There are about 170 billion galaxies in the universe. And each galaxy is full of billions of stars. Some galaxies are near, and others are very, very far away. Astronomers can barely see them when they look through the most powerful telescopes. If you took a spaceship past the farthest star in the farthest galaxy, you would find empty space that goes on forever.

Guess what? God is bigger than that. Solomon said, "Not even the highest of heavens can hold God" (2 Chronicles 2:6 ICB). God is everywhere in the universe with every star. He also fills all the empty space beyond the edge of the farthest galaxies.

The Bible says, "God is love" (1 John 4:8 NKJV). Imagine you could go past the edge of the universe, past the last lonely star. You would still find your caring God there. And He would still hold you close.

David said, "Where can I go from your Spirit? Where can I flee from your presence? If I go up to the heavens, you are there; if I make my bed in the depths, you are there. If I rise on the wings of the dawn, if I settle on the far side of the sea, even there your hand will guide me, your right hand will hold me fast'" (Psalm 139:7–10 NIV).

"The LORD says, 'Heaven is my throne, and the earth is my footstool'" (Isaiah 66:1 GNT). A footstool is a short, small stool that someone rests their feet on when they sit in a big living room chair or on a king's throne. This verse doesn't mean God actually rests his feet on the North Pole. That's *not* why the Arctic ice is melting. It simply means that God is so huge that our entire planet is very small to Him.

God knows that it's hard for you to imagine Him being so big. That's why He came down to earth as a man, as Jesus, the Son of God. He did it so that you could relate to Him and understand Him better.

Do you understand how God could be so big?

Does it matter if you can't?

How does learning how big God is help you understand how powerful He is?

3. HOW CAN GOD KNOW EVERYTHING?

\\\\\\\\\\\\\\\\\\\

The short answer is God can know everything because He's God.

But here's a longer answer: You can't know everything because your mind is so much smaller than God's mind. Your mind is only a little bigger than a softball, but God's mind is far bigger than you can even imagine. He can think of everything that has ever happened, everything that is happening now, and everything that will ever happen.

A lot of people try to figure that out. But they still can't understand it. Then they say that God doesn't make sense. That's like saying that your math teacher makes no sense because you can't understand what she's teaching. The fact is, she's very smart. You just don't understand the math problem she's explaining.

Have you ever seen a movie or a TV show where a scientist is standing in front of a whiteboard full of long equations? The scientist is a genius and understands those equations. But you say, "All I know is 2 + 2 = 4. I can't make sense of his big equation. So because I can't understand it, it must be nonsense."

What would the other students do if you said *that* out loud in class? They'd probably all burst out laughing.

The Bible says, "Our Lord is great and very

powerful. There is no limit to what he knows" (Psalm 147:5 ICB). Another Bible translation says, "Great and mighty is our Lord; his wisdom cannot be measured" (GNT). There is a limit to *your* understanding, however. That's why you're in the grade that you're in, and not in the next one. And your understanding and wisdom *can* be measured. Teachers measure them by asking you questions and by giving you tests. This gives them an idea of what you know and don't know.

" 'My thoughts are nothing like your thoughts,' says the LORD. 'And my ways are far beyond anything you could imagine. For just as the heavens are higher than the earth, so my ways are higher than your ways and my thoughts higher than your thoughts'" (Isaiah 55:8–9 NLT).

God designed all the amazing living creatures on this planet. He even designed the law of gravity. He's so incredibly smart! You can't possibly understand Someone who knows absolutely everything. You may ask, "How can God know everything? His mind would have to be enormous!" And guess what? It is! Maybe now you understand why God is so *big*!

A genius is much smarter than you. How much smarter is God than a genius?

What questions do you have? Who knows the answers to them all?

4. DID GOD HAVE A MOM AND A DAD?

\\\\\\\\\\\\\\\\\\\\\\\\\

Good question! Lots of kids ask this one. In fact, when I was young, I asked my grandpa the same question.

Why do you wonder such things? Probably because everything you can think of has a beginning and an ending. You know from nature shows that lions give birth to lion cubs, and elephants give birth to baby elephants. And cats have kittens and baby birds hatch from eggs. You were once a baby too. You celebrate the day you were born with a birthday party.

So you may wonder if God had a beginning too. Did He have a mom and a dad? But if the Lord had a mother and a father, then *they* would have been God before He was born. Then God wouldn't be the only God. But no one was around before Him. The Lord tells us, "I alone am God. There is no other God—there never has been, and there never will be" (Isaiah 43:10 NLT).

So where did He come from? Well, He has always been. If you could go way, way, way back in time, you would find that God was always there. He is called "the living God." That's because He has always *been* living and always *will* live. He has no beginning, and He has no ending. He was never born, and He will never die. Millions of people are born, live their lives, then die. But God lasts forever.

If you don't understand how that works, don't worry. If you could understand everything, you'd be as smart as God. And no person can know as much as God. Right?

You may also have wondered if God has brothers and sisters. The ancient Greeks believed that their "gods" had families just like people. Their fathers and mothers quarreled and fought, and their children did terrible things to each other. But in the Bible God says very clearly: "There is no other God. . . . I am the only One" (Isaiah 44:8 icb). So God doesn't have any brothers and sisters.

Many people in the world *say* there are lots of gods. But Christians know that there's only one God. These other gods aren't real. They're just made up. Some people worship things as gods. For example, they worship the sun. But it's not a god. A wise man once said that "there is one God, and there is no other but He" (Mark 12:32 nkjv).

How do you know God doesn't have parents, or brothers and sisters?

What did the Greeks say their gods had families like? "Just like ___."

5. WHAT DOES GOD LOOK LIKE?

\\\\\\\\\\\\\\\\\\\\\\\\\\\

Many people think God looks like an old man with a long, white beard and white hair. They believe He has a face, eyes, ears, nose, and mouth—and a body with arms and legs—just like us. And they picture Him wearing white robes, just like men in Bible days wore. Where do people get these ideas?

They get them from the Bible. The prophet Daniel said, "I watched as thrones were put in place and the Ancient One sat down to judge. His clothing was as white as snow, his hair like purest wool" (Daniel 7:9 NLT).

But remember: God is bigger than the whole universe, so we could never see all of Him at once. The Bible says that "the heavens, even the highest heavens, cannot contain him" (2 Chronicles 2:6 NIV). Daniel saw God sitting on a great throne in heaven, in a human-looking body. But God still filled the entire universe.

What does this mean? It means that God was in a body and—at the same time—He was still everywhere outside that body. You can't do something that amazing. You're in one place in one body, and that's the only place you can be. But God can be in one special place—like on His throne in heaven—and still be everywhere else.

It's impossible for humans, but God does it all the time.

We don't know how He does it, but we know why He does it. He does it to relate to us. He knows we can't look everywhere at once to see Him. And He knows we're most comfortable seeing other humans. So He appears on His throne in heaven in a human-looking body.

Just because God appears in a human body, doesn't mean He's our size. God is huge! Moses once prayed, "Now, please show me your greatness." God answered, "But you cannot see my face. No one can see me and stay alive." Then God said, "There is a place near me where you may stand on a rock. My greatness will pass that place. I will put you in a large crack in that rock. And I will cover you with my hand until I have passed by. Then I will take away my hand, and you will see my back. But my face must not be seen" (Exodus 33:18, 20–23 ICB). God had to have huge hands to cover the whole opening Moses was standing in.

Do you think God looks like an old man with a white beard and a robe? Why?

Why did God often appear to people in a human-looking body?

6. WHY DO SOME PEOPLE SAY THERE IS NO GOD?

\\\\\\\\\\\\\\\\\\\\\\\\\\\\

The Bible says, "Only fools say in their hearts, 'There is no God' " (Psalm 14:1 NLT). Some people insist that they won't believe in anything they can't see, hear, smell, taste, or touch. It really bothers them that they can't find God with their physical senses. The funny thing is, these same people believe in gravity, even though they can't see it. But gravity keeps on working even when people are foolish enough *not* to believe in it. Why? Because it's real.

You may have noticed that 99.999% of the time, God can't be seen. In fact, the apostle Paul calls Him "the invisible God" (Colossians 1:15 GNT). That's just the way He normally is. Moses "kept his eyes on the one who is invisible" (Hebrews 11:27 NLT). He couldn't see God, but he kept on following Him. He trusted that God was there just the same.

You must do the same thing. "For we live by believing and not by seeing" (2 Corinthians 5:7 NLT). You can't see God, but you can believe He's there. You know He's there because He protects you, gives you peace and love, and supplies what you need. He does small miracles for you every day. The fact that God answers prayer proves that He's real. It shows that He's close to you and is watching over you.

Often, people sin or don't pay any attention to God for a long time. Then He may remove *all* signs that He's there. He stops answering their prayers—usually because they're no longer praying. So God hides from them. This forces people to search for Him, and they cry out, "God, where are You?"

You may ask, "Does God *actually* hide Himself?" Well, odd as this may sound, the answer is yes. Isaiah wrote, "Truly You *are* God, who hide Yourself, O God of Israel" (Isaiah 45:15 NKJV). Another translation says, "The God of Israel. . .is a God who conceals himself" (GNT).

Many Christians talk about "seeking God." By this they mean to pray until they feel that God is near. The apostle Paul said God's "purpose was for the nations to seek after God and perhaps feel their way toward him and find him—though he is not far from any one of us" (Acts 17:27 NLT). Often, people seek God only for a brief time. They don't keep at it until they truly find Him. So keep seeking God until you're sure He's there.

How easy or how hard is it for you to trust the invisible God?

Do you feel very close to God sometimes?
  Or far away other times?

7. WHY SHOULD I FEAR GOD IF "GOD IS LOVE"?

\\\\\\\\\\\\\\\\\\\\\\\\\\\\\\

The Bible says many times that believers are supposed to fear God. In fact, it says "God is greatly to be feared" (Psalm 89:7 NKJV). And Jesus said, "Do not be afraid of those who kill the body but cannot kill the soul; rather be afraid of God, who can destroy both body and soul in hell" (Matthew 10:28 GNT).

But isn't God your Father who looks on you with love? Yes, that's true. And the Bible says, "God is love." Plus it says, "There is no fear in love" (1 John 4:8, 18 NKJV). So you may ask, "Why should I fear God?"

First of all, let's understand what the Bible means when it says to "fear God." King Solomon said, "The fear of the LORD is the beginning of wisdom" (Proverbs 9:10 NKJV). But another translation translates it this way: "Wisdom begins with respect for the Lord" (ICB). You must respect the Lord and worship Him. And you must be in awe of Him, because He truly is awesome.

Siberian tigers are the biggest, most dangerous cats on this planet. A male Siberian tiger can weigh 850 pounds. That's 100 pounds heavier than an African lion. And these awesome beasts, with their beautiful orange and white fur with black stripes, are deadly. They're dangerous. You do *not* want to be alone in a room with them. You respect them, all right. You fear them. You'd be crazy if you didn't.

But what if you're a *tiger cub*, and that ferocious Siberian tiger is your *dad*? Well now, that changes everything. And you have that kind of relationship with God. You're His son or daughter. You still must respect the Lord, be in awe of Him, and worship Him. You are to fear Him. But fearing God is not a negative thing. In fact, the Bible says, "The fear of the LORD is pure" (Psalm 19:9 NIV).

To fear God means to be afraid to disobey Him. If your dad warns you that you'll be grounded for a week if you come home late, you're going to be afraid to break his rule. God won't harm you, but He will discipline you. A tiger cub may play with his dad and wrestle with his tail. But if that cub does something wrong, he finds out real quick who's boss.

There will be times in your life when God shows His great power. So make sure you respect Him.

- -

How much do you respect and fear God?
  Are you in awe of Him?

How is fear of something powerful and
  dangerous, a good thing?

8. HOW CAN JESUS BE GOD IF GOD IS HIS FATHER?

\\\\\\\\\\\\\\\\\\\\\\\

Luke 6:12 (NLT) says, "Jesus went up on a mountain to pray, and he prayed to God all night." So some people ask, "If Jesus is God, was He just praying to Himself?" They mostly ask this because they think it's a very clever question. But it *is* a good question, so let's look at the answer.

There is one, true God. He is made up of the Father, the Son, and the Holy Spirit. We call this the Trinity. He's one God, but He exists as three Persons—and one of those Persons is Jesus Christ, God the Son.

Does the Bible *say* Jesus is God? Yes, it does. The Gospel of John says, "In the beginning the Word already existed. The Word was with God, and the Word was God." And John says, "The Word became human" (John 1:1, 14 NLT). It's clearly talking about Jesus. John 1:18 (NLT) says, "But the unique One [Jesus], who is himself God, is near to the Father's heart."

Genesis 1:1 (NLT) says, "In the beginning God created the heavens and the earth." Got that? *God* created everything! But Hebrews 1:2 (NLT) says, "through the Son he created the universe."

Jesus prayed to God the Father. But His Father also calls *Jesus* "God." The Bible says, "And when he brought his supreme Son into the world, God said, 'Let all of God's angels worship him.'. . . But to the Son he says, 'Your throne, O God, endures forever and ever. You rule with a scepter of justice. . . . Therefore, O God, your God [the Father] has anointed you'" (Hebrews 1:6, 8–9 NLT).

How could Jesus become an ordinary man if He was God? God is all-powerful and bigger than the universe. How could God fit into a small, weak human body without causing it to explode? Easy, Jesus let go of all His mighty power. He left it in heaven.

"Though he was God, he did not think of equality with God as something to cling to. Instead, he gave up his divine privileges; he. . .was born as a human being. . . . And died a criminal's death on a cross" (Philippians 2:6–8 NLT). When Jesus became a human being, he didn't hang on to His God-power. He let go of it and was born in a weak body as a normal baby. God can't die, but Jesus' body *could* die. . .and did.

Could you now explain to someone else how Jesus is God? Try it.

What did Jesus have to leave in heaven to be born an ordinary baby?

9. WHAT DOES JESUS LOOK LIKE?

\\\\\\\\\\\\\\\\\\\\\\\\\\

When I was a young boy going to Sunday School, almost all the pictures showed Jesus with white skin, blond hair, and blue eyes. That was the way people thought He looked. At least, that was how they *wanted* Him to look. In those days, ads on TV told women to color their hair blond. They said, "Blonds have more fun!" Shampoo commercials often showed women with beautiful, shiny, blond hair. So many people said, "Huh! Jesus looks like He belongs in a shampoo commercial."

Then people began asking, "But wasn't Jesus a Jew? So why doesn't He look Jewish?" It made no sense. Most Jews in Jesus' day had light brown skin and brown eyes. And their hair was black and often curly. Now, many modern Jews are fair-skinned and some even have blond hair. But that's because their ancestors married Europeans.

It took a few years, but finally artists began drawing Jesus looking more Jewish. No one really knows exactly what He looked like though. So pictures of Him today are still just an artist's imagination. But most of them are more realistic. Some still make Him look almost blond though.

Some people think that Jesus wasn't very good-looking, because Isaiah prophesied: "My servant grew up in the LORD's presence like a tender green shoot, like a root in dry ground. There was nothing beautiful or majestic about his appearance, nothing to attract us to him" (Isaiah 53:2 NLT). Maybe Jesus wasn't good-looking. But Isaiah had just described Him as "a root in dry ground." So he could have been talking about how a dry root looked. We don't really know.

Some people believe that Jesus was black. They point out that the Bible says His hair was "like wool" (Revelation 1:14 NLT). But the full verse says, "His head and his hair were white like wool, as white as snow." But that wasn't how Jesus looked in His natural body. That was how He looked after He rose from the dead and had a glorious *new* body. Read this to see how majestic Jesus looks *now*:

"His head and his hair were white like wool, as white as snow. And his eyes were like flames of fire. His feet were like polished bronze refined in a furnace, and his voice thundered like mighty ocean waves. . . . And his face was like the sun in all its brilliance" (Revelation 1:14–16 NLT).

And remember: what was in Jesus' heart was far more important than how He looked on the outside.

What do you think Jesus looked like?

Jesus was Jewish. What did most Jews back then look like?

10. DOES JESUS HAVE BROTHERS AND SISTERS?

\\\\\\\\\\\\\\\\\\\\\\\\\\

Yes, Jesus had four brothers and several sisters. Jesus grew up in Nazareth, but later He traveled all over Israel, teaching people. When Jesus returned to Nazareth people said, "His mother is Mary. His brothers are James, Joseph, Simon and Judas. And all his sisters are here with us" (Matthew 13:55–56 icb).

This verse tells us the name of Jesus' four brothers, but we don't know the names of His sisters. There were probably three or more girls, because the Bible talks about "*all* his sisters." That's for *sure* more than one, and it even sounds like more than two.

Some Christians believe Mary didn't have any more children after Jesus. They think that Joseph had been married before and had several children with his first wife. After she died, Joseph married again. His new wife, Mary, had just one son, Jesus. Is that what happened? We don't know. But we *do* know that Jesus was "her firstborn Son" (Matthew 1:25 nkjv). So if Mary had several children, Jesus was the oldest child. If Jesus was Mary's *only* son, then He was the youngest child.

Jesus sometimes had problems with His family. At first, His brothers didn't believe God had sent Him to save the world. Once, Jesus' enemies in Judea wanted to kill Him. But Jesus' brothers mocked Him: "Leave here and go to Judea. . . ! You can't become famous if you hide like this!" (John 7:3–4 NLT).

Another time, Jesus went in a house to eat, and a large crowd *squeeeezed* in around Him. People were packed so close together that Jesus couldn't eat. So He began to teach them. Jesus' family heard that people were saying, "He is out of his mind." So they wanted to grab Jesus and take Him home to Nazareth.

The crowd told Him, "Your mother and brothers are waiting for you outside." Jesus asked, "Who is my mother? Who are my brothers?" Then Jesus looked at those sitting around him. He said, "Here are my mother and my brothers! My true brother and sister and mother are those who do the things God wants" (Mark 3:21, 32–35 ICB).

Of course, James, Joseph, Simon, and Judas were still Jesus' brothers. But Jesus meant that people like you are *also* His brothers and sisters. Do you squeeze in real close to Jesus to hear His stories? Do you do what God tells you to do? Then you're Jesus' brother or sister!

Do you think Jesus was the oldest or the youngest child? Which are you?

Do you have problems with *your* brothers or sisters? How do you work them out?

11. WHO IS THE HOLY SPIRIT?

\\\\\\\\\\\\\\\\\\\\\

In the Trinity, there's God the Father, God the Son, and God the Holy Spirit. So Christians often say that the Holy Spirit is "the Third Person of the Trinity."

Some people forget that the Holy Spirit is an actual Person. They think the Spirit is an "it." They imagine He's just a kind of power or energy that Jesus used. They don't understand verses like these: "The angel answered, 'The Holy Spirit will come on you, and God's power will rest upon you'" (Luke 1:35 GNT). "Then Jesus returned to Galilee, and the power of the Holy Spirit was with him" (Luke 4:14 GNT).

These verses don't say that the Holy Spirit is just some kind of power like electricity. When it says, "the power of the Holy Spirit," it means that the Holy Spirit *has* power, God's power. And the Spirit gave that power to Jesus. God the Father has the same power—enough to create the entire universe!

When God's Spirit comes into your life, you too will have power. That's a promise. "The Holy Spirit will come to you. Then you will receive power" (Acts 1:8 ICB).

Here are some verses that show that the Holy Spirit is a Person: the Holy Spirit loves people (Romans 15:30); He becomes grieved (sad) when believers disobey (Ephesians 4:30); sometimes He becomes insulted (Hebrews 10:29); people may lie to Him (Acts 5:3–4, 9); and He has a mind (Romans 8:27).

The Holy Spirit causes people to be born again. People are "born of the Spirit" (John 3:8 NLT) when He comes into their life. The Spirit is overflowing with power and life, so He gives eternal life to everyone He touches. When He enters a person's heart, He causes their sinful, dead spirit to come to life. Because He is holy, whenever He comes into a person's heart, He makes them holy.

The Holy Spirit gives people spiritual gifts, talents, and abilities. "The Spirit gives one person the ability to speak with wisdom. And the same Spirit gives another the ability to speak with knowledge. The same Spirit gives faith to one person. And that one Spirit gives another gifts of healing. The Spirit gives to another person the power to do miracles, to another the ability to prophesy. And he gives to another the ability to know the difference between good and evil spirits. . . . One Spirit, the same Spirit, does all these things. The Spirit decides what to give each person." (1 Corinthians 12:8–11 ICB).

Can you explain to someone who the Holy Spirit is? Try it now.

How do you know the Spirit isn't just an "it"— some kind of power?

12. WHY DID JESUS PICK JUDAS TO BE HIS DISCIPLE?

\\\\\\\\\\\\\\\\\\\\\\\\\

Jesus had been traveling around Galilee for many months, teaching and healing. A great crowd of disciples, including many women, followed Him (see Luke 8:1–3).

One day, "Jesus went up on a mountain to pray, and he prayed to God all night. At daybreak he called together all of his disciples and chose twelve of them to be apostles. Here are their names: Simon (whom he named Peter), Andrew (Peter's brother), James, John, Philip, Bartholomew, Matthew, Thomas, James (son of Alphaeus), Simon (who was called the zealot), Judas (son of James), Judas Iscariot (who later betrayed him)" (Luke 6:12–16 NLT).

The question some people have is, "Why did Jesus choose an evil man as one of His closest disciples? Jesus prayed about His choices. Didn't God tell Him what Judas would do?"

Jesus *did* know. Later He said, "'I chose the twelve of you, didn't I? Yet one of you is a devil!' He was talking about Judas, the son of Simon Iscariot" (John 6:70–71 GNT). This was a year before Judas betrayed Him. So Jesus knew what was in Judas' heart. He probably knew from the beginning that Judas would betray Him. That may be the reason Jesus prayed *all night*. He didn't *want* to pick Judas. But someone had to betray Jesus to His enemies.

While they were eating the Last Supper, Jesus said, "I tell you that one of you will betray me—one who is eating with me." Then Jesus told them, "The Son of Man will die as the Scriptures say he will; but how terrible for that man who will betray the Son of Man! It would have been better for that man if he had never been born!" (Mark 14:18, 21 GNT).

After Judas led the mob to Jesus, Peter tried to stop them from arresting Him. But Jesus told Peter to put his sword away. He said that if God *wanted* to, God could send an army of angels to protect Him. Jesus asked, "But if I did, how would the Scriptures be fulfilled that describe what must happen now?" (Matthew 26:54 NLT).

God prophesied that one of the Savior's disciples would betray Him (see Psalm 41:9; John 13:18). And Jesus knew that Judas would turn on Him. That doesn't mean that what Judas did was right. But it had to happen. Otherwise, Jesus wouldn't have died on the cross for the sins of the world.

Why did Jesus *have* to pick Judas as one of His closest disciples?

Did Jesus really want Judas as His close disciple?

13. HOW COULD JESUS WALK ON WATER?

\\\\\\\\\\\\\\\\\\\\\\\\\\\

One time, Jesus' twelve disciples were in a boat far from land. They were crossing the Sea of Galilee in the middle of the night. A strong wind had risen, and they were fighting heavy waves. It must have been like riding down white-water rapids. Things were bad enough already. Then they saw someone coming toward them, walking on the water. The disciples became *really* scared. They cried out, "It's a ghost!"

But it was Jesus. And He said, "Don't be afraid. Take courage. I am here!" Then Peter said, "Lord, if it's really you, tell me to come to you, walking on the water." Jesus said, "Yes, come." So Peter stepped out of the boat and walked on the water toward Jesus. But when he saw the strong waves, he was terrified and began to sink. He shouted, "Save me, Lord!" Jesus reached out and grabbed him. "You have so little faith," He said. "Why did you doubt me?" When they climbed back into the boat, the wind stopped (Matthew 14:26–31 NLT).

Now, think about it: Jesus was not only walking on water, but on *wild* water. A storm was raging. Waves were rushing across the lake, rapidly rising and falling. Jesus was not only staying on top of the water, but was keeping His balance. He didn't slip and fall over. It must have been like riding a bucking bronco. That's what sunk Peter. He could handle walking on water. But when he saw the strong wind and the waves, he was scared.

How did Jesus *do* it? We don't know, because the Bible doesn't say. But would you like to hear some guesses? Remember what the disciples shouted. Before Jesus got close enough for them to recognize Him, they yelled, "It's a ghost!" They knew that ghosts weigh nothing and don't sink in water. So God possibly surrounded Jesus with antigravity energy. Then He didn't sink. God once did a miracle like this with an iron ax head (see 2 Kings 6:1–7).

Insects called Water Striders walk on water. God gave them very light bodies and special, long legs that don't sink. They can stand on top of water because the surface tension holds them up. "Surface tension" is the way the top of the water acts like a thin plastic sheet. So who knows? Maybe *that's* the way God did this miracle. Maybe He made the water's surface tension extra strong under Jesus' feet.

Even if we *can't* understand how God did a miracle, did He do it anyway?

How do *you* think Jesus and Peter walked on the water?

14. WHY DID PEOPLE HATE JESUS WHEN HE WAS SO GOOD?

\\\\\\\\\\\\\\\\\\\\\\\\

Jesus was a very good man. In fact, He was perfect. He always obeyed His heavenly Father. And He was always doing good, and teaching people to love one another. So why did the religious leaders hate Him? They called Jesus "that liar" (Matthew 27:63 GNT). Why did they think He was a liar?

Well, let's look at what ordinary Jews said about Jesus: "Some argued, 'He's a good man,' but others said, 'He's nothing but a fraud who deceives the people'" (John 7:12 NLT). If you went by what Jesus did and said, you got the idea He was a good man. Nicodemus said, "No one could perform the miracles you are doing unless God were with him" (John 3:2 GNT). However, the religious leaders argued that you had to look deeper. Then you'd see that Jesus was only *pretending* to be good.

Why did they not see the wonderful miracles Jesus was doing? Why did they ignore His good teachings? Because, in their opinion, He didn't keep the Sabbath. They were angry that Jesus often "worked" on the day of rest. They argued, "This man does not keep the Sabbath day. He is not from God!" (John 9:16 ICB).

The Law of Moses stated, "You must keep

the day of rest, because it is sacred. Whoever does not keep it, but works on that day, is to be put to death" (Exodus 31:14 GNT). So the religious leaders argued that Jesus was a bad person. They insisted that He should be killed.

Most of the time, Jesus and His disciples rested on the Sabbath. For example, He only healed people *after* the Sabbath ended at sundown (Mark 1:21, 32–34). But the Pharisees had added thousands of tiny rules to Moses' Law. They said that many harmless, good activities were "work." But Jesus didn't follow their man-made laws. He sometimes healed a sick person on the Sabbath. So they argued that He wasn't of God.

"Then a demon-possessed man, who was blind and couldn't speak, was brought to Jesus. He healed the man so that he could both speak and see. The crowd was amazed and asked, 'Could it be that Jesus is. . .the Messiah?' But when the Pharisees heard about the miracle, they said, 'No wonder he can cast out demons. He gets his power from Satan, the prince of demons'" (Matthew 12:22–24 NLT).

As you can see, the religious leaders were very badly mixed-up.

- -

Why did the religious leaders say Jesus was a liar?

Why did they argue that Jesus didn't keep the Sabbath?

15. WHY DID JESUS HAVE TO DIE?

\\\\\\\\\\\\\\\\\\\\\\\\\\

Many people think that Jesus was a great teacher who taught good things like loving others. So they don't understand why He had to die. They think it was a terrible thing. Other people think Jesus was a prophet who warned people against living selfishly. They think He died because He had so many enemies.

But Jesus had to die because He was the Lamb of God. John the Baptist said, "There is the Lamb of God, who takes away the sin of the world!" (John 1:29 GNT). How did Jesus do that? Ever since God created Adam and Eve, and they disobeyed, people have sinned. And "the payment for sin is death" (Romans 6:23 ICB).

This is not just people's bodies dying. It's their spirits *and* their bodies dying in hell. It's eternal separation from God. It's missing out on eternal life. People needed to be saved. What could they do? Well, instead of them dying for their sins, God allowed people to sacrifice lambs. When the lamb was killed, its blood flowed out. God accepted that as payment for the death people deserved.

The problem was that people kept sinning. So they were always offering lambs as sacrifices. But it was never enough.

Before the world began, God knew people would sin. So He made a solution. He planned to send His only Son, Jesus Christ, as the perfect Lamb, to die once for sin. "Now when all ages of time are nearing the end, he has appeared. . . to remove sin through the sacrifice of himself" (Hebrews 9:26 GNT). Then, whoever believed in Jesus could find *total* forgiveness for *all* their sins. They could be saved from hell.

How do you receive forgiveness of sins? How do you get eternal life in heaven? It's simple. Pray: "Dear God, I've sinned against You and others and deserve death. But I thank You that You provided a Lamb to die in my place—Your Son, Jesus. I thank You that His blood pays the price for all my sins. I believe that He died on the cross for me. And I believe that He rose from the dead and lives forever. Please send the Spirit of Your Son into my heart. Make me Your child. In Jesus' name, I ask. Amen."

If you prayed this prayer sincerely, you're now God's child. You're saved, and you have an eternal home in heaven. That's wonderful news! Be sure to tell others about it.

Have you asked God to send Jesus into your heart?

Can you explain to someone else why Jesus had to die?

16. HOW COULD JESUS BE ALIVE AFTER HE WAS DEAD?

\\\\\\\\\\\\\\\\\\\\\\

Most people, once they die, *stay* dead. Every so often, you will hear of someone who was only dead for ten or twenty minutes. Their heart stopped beating, and they no longer breathed. Their body began to get cold. Then a doctor did something that brought them back to life. But eventually, that person will die again. And next time they *won't* come back to life.

But Jesus was dead for *three days*! Plus, the Roman soldiers had beat Him savagely. They whipped Him again and again with a cat-o'-nine-tails. This whip sliced open His back, His arms, and His legs. He had lost much blood. No doctor on earth could have brought Jesus back. He was definitely dead.

But God's Holy Spirit brought Jesus' body back to life. In fact, He did much *more* than that. The Holy Spirit didn't just raise Jesus back to life for a few more years. The Holy Spirit completely changed Jesus' body. It had died as a weak earthly body. Now it was a powerful, eternal body. Something that is "eternal" lives forever and ever.

In the question, "What does Jesus look like?" we quoted verses from Revelation 1. These verses show you what Jesus looks like now with His new, eternal body. Remember them? Read them again.

Jesus now looks absolutely fantastic! His face, His hands, His feet, His entire body, glow with great power.

It's the same body Jesus had on earth, but it's no longer mortal. It's immortal. When we say something is "mortal" we mean that it will die. "Immortal" means it can never die. Jesus' body, full of power, light, and glory, will live for all eternity—forever and ever.

And there's good news for us too: one day *our* weak, earthly bodies will be changed just like Jesus' body was. "The Spirit of God, who raised Jesus from the dead, lives in you. And just as God raised Christ Jesus from the dead, he will give life to your mortal bodies by this same Spirit living within you" (Romans 8:11 NLT).

Paul said, "While we live in these earthly bodies, we groan and sigh, but it's not that we want to die and get rid of these bodies that clothe us. Rather, we want to put on our new bodies so that these dying bodies will be swallowed up by life" (2 Corinthians 5:4 NLT).

Did God bring Jesus back to life for a few years? For how long?

You will one day be immortal. How does that make you feel?

17. IS JESUS THE ONLY WAY TO HEAVEN?

\\\\\\\\\\\\\\\\\\\\\\\\\\\\\\\\\

Yes, Jesus, God's Son, is the only way to heaven. The only way you'll live forever with God, your Father, is if you trust in Jesus. "For God loved the world so much that he gave his only Son. God gave his Son so that whoever believes in him may not be lost, but have eternal life" (John 3:16 ICB).

But your neighbor down the street may say, "Well, yes. You can have eternal life by believing in Jesus. But He's not the *only* way to heaven. You can also have eternal life if you believe in Buddha, Muhammad, or Vishnu." Or you might have an aunt or uncle who says, "No matter *what* god or idol you pray to, you'll be saved. As long as you're a good person, you'll go to heaven."

Many people believe these kinds of things. But just because they believe something, doesn't mean they're right. In fact, they're wrong. Jesus is not only *a* way to heaven. He's *the* way—the *only* way. Jesus Himself said, "I am the way. And I am the truth and the life. The only way to the Father is through me" (John 14:6 ICB).

The apostle Peter told a huge crowd of people, "Jesus is the only One who can save people. No one else in the world is able to save us" (Acts 4:12 ICB). Do you know what that means? It means that no other god or idol or religious leader in the world can save you. Only Jesus Christ, God's Son, can. And why is that?

Other religious teachers may teach *some* good things. They may say *some* things that are true. They don't say wrong things *all* the time. But Jesus was the only person in the world who told the truth all the time. And He's the only one who died for your sins. Remember what we told you earlier about Jesus being the Lamb of God? Jesus was the only one who ever died to save you.

And Jesus didn't *stay* dead. He rose again after He died, and now He sits on the right hand of God's throne in heaven—alive forever and ever. All the other religious teachers and so-called prophets died. . .and they *stayed* dead.

Put your trust in Jesus, God's one and only Son. Only He can save you! And don't argue with other people who don't believe in Jesus. They're wrong, but they're still free to believe what they want.

What is the only way to get to heaven?

Can you be saved by following *any* religious
    leader? Why or why not?

18. WHAT DOES JESUS DO IN HEAVEN?

\\\\\\\\\\\\\\\\\\\\\\\\\\\\

Jesus is at the very center of all power in the universe. He sits at the right hand of the throne of God in heaven. You may wonder if He just sits there talking to God His Father and the angels. But Jesus is incredibly busy. He's doing more things at once than you could possibly imagine. Don't forget: Jesus isn't just a man. He's God. And now that He's back in heaven, He has all of His astonishing power back.

Jesus now fills the entire universe. He holds all things together and keeps all the billions of galaxies running. The Bible says: "The one who came down is the same one who went up, above and beyond the heavens, to fill the whole universe with his presence" (Ephesians 4:10 GNT). The Bible also says: "Everything was created through him and for him. He existed before anything else, and he holds all creation together" (Colossians 1:16–17 NLT).

Jesus also sends His Spirit into the heart of every person on earth who believes in Him. He said, "I will send you the Helper from the Father. He is the Spirit of truth who comes from the Father" (John 15:26 ICB). Jesus also sends His Spirit to give people special gifts and abilities. "There are different kinds of gifts; but they are all from the same Spirit. . . . And there are different ways that God works in people; but all these ways are from the same God. God works in us all in everything we do. Something from the Spirit can be seen in each person, to help everyone" (1 Corinthians 12:4, 6–7 ICB).

Jesus is with you all the time, even when you sin. When the devil comes to accuse you, Jesus pleads with His Father to have mercy. He reminds God that even though you've been disobedient, you're still His child. "And so he is able, now and always, to save those who come to God through him, because he lives forever to plead with God for them" (Hebrews 7:25 GNT).

Jesus also greets every Christian who dies and goes to heaven. Just before a man named Stephen died, He saw Jesus. Jesus had risen from His throne and was coming to welcome him. "But Stephen. . .looked up to heaven and saw God's glory and Jesus standing at the right side of God. 'Look!' he said. 'I see heaven opened and the Son of Man standing at the right side of God!'" (Acts 7:55–56 GNT).

How many things does Jesus do in heaven?

How is it possible for Jesus to do so much at
  once?

19. HOW CAN JESUS LIVE IN MY HEART?

\\\\\\\\\\\\\\\\\\\\\\\\\

Christians often talk about Jesus living in their heart. Does Jesus actually live in someone's heart? After all, the Bible says that He's sitting on a throne on the right hand of His Father's throne in heaven. The apostle Mark wrote, "When the Lord Jesus had finished talking with them [the apostles], he was taken up into heaven and sat down in the place of honor at God's right hand" (Mark 16:19 NLT).

How can Jesus be sitting on a throne in heaven *and* be living in the hearts of millions of Christians at once, all around the world? Simple. He does it through the power of the Holy Spirit. Jesus promised, "The Helper will come—the Spirit, who reveals the truth about God and who comes from the Father. I will send him to you from the Father" (John 15:26 GNT).

In another place, the Bible says, "And you are God's children. That is why God sent the Spirit of his Son into your hearts. The Spirit cries out, 'Father, dear Father'" (Galatians 4:6 ICB). Remember, the Father, the Son, and the Holy Spirit are all one God. The Holy Spirit is the Spirit of Jesus, and God the Father sends the Spirit into your heart.

The apostle Paul wrote, "I ask the Father. . .to

give you the power to be strong in spirit. He will give you that strength through his Spirit. I pray that Christ will live in your hearts because of your faith" (Ephesians 3:16–17 ICB). So you see, the Holy Spirit *and* Jesus live in your heart if you're God's child.

Paul called the Holy Spirit "the Spirit of Christ." He said, "You are ruled by the Spirit, if that Spirit of God really lives in you. But if anyone does not have the Spirit of Christ, then he does not belong to Christ" (Romans 8:9 ICB). Also, remember, the Bible talks about your "heart." It's not saying that God lives in the heart in your chest that pumps blood through your body. It means God lives deep in your mind and spirit.

It's not enough to just agree that there is a God and that Jesus is real. "Do you believe that there is only one God? Good! The demons also believe—and tremble with fear" (James 2:19 GNT). They tremble with fear because they hate Him and disobey Him. They know He is going to punish them someday. You not only need to believe in God and Jesus; you have to love Them also.

- -

What does the Bible mean when it says that Jesus lives in your heart?

Besides believing in Jesus, what must you do to be saved?

20. WHAT DOES IT MEAN TO BE "BORN AGAIN"?

\\\\\\\\\\\\\\\\\\\\\\\\\\\\

Jesus said, "Unless you are born again, you cannot be in God's kingdom" (John 3:3 ICB). What does "born again" mean? When Jesus said this to an old man named Nicodemus, he asked Jesus, "But if a man is already old, how can he be born again? He cannot enter his mother's body again. So how can he be born a second time?" (v. 4).

Nicodemus misunderstood Jesus. That's not what Jesus was talking about. You're born again when the Spirit of Christ enters you and fills you with the life of God. "God has sent the Spirit of his Son into our hearts." And "The Spirit alone gives eternal life" (Galatians 4:6; John 6:63 NLT).

Being saved is more than simply believing something. It's more than agreeing that God exists and that Jesus died to save you. Being saved is when you open your heart to the Holy Spirit. Then He comes with His mighty power and plugs you in to God. The apostle Paul tells you that "he who is joined to the Lord is one spirit *with Him*" (1 Corinthians 6:17 NKJV). When you're united with God, you have *His* life in you—eternal life.

Many people imagine that God is looking down from far away in heaven. They think He is completely separate from people. Then, when you give your heart to Him, He writes your name in the Book of Life—and you're saved. But if you do something bad to "break the contract," He glances your way, scratches out your name, and goes back to His business. That's *not* how it is at all!

When you open your heart to Him, God sends His Spirit to live inside you. God sent the Spirit of His Son to bring light and life in your heart. When that happens, you are "born of the Spirit" (John 3:8 GNT). The Spirit of Christ personally dwells in your heart, and your spirit is united with His Spirit.

The Bible says that "if Christ is in you. . .the Spirit gives life" (Romans 8:10 NIV). So what gives you salvation? The fact that you believe in God and love Him? Yes, these things open the door so that His Spirit can enter your heart. This makes your spirit come alive, and gives you eternal life. Remember, the Spirit gives life.

The opposite is also true. "If anyone does not have the Spirit of Christ, he is not His" (Romans 8:9 NKJV).

How is a person "born again" or "born of the Spirit"?

What gives you life—eternal life?

21. DO I HAVE TO BE GOOD TO GO TO HEAVEN?

\\\\\\\\\\\\\\\\\\\\\\\\\

Many Christians think that Jesus doesn't actually save them. They think that He came to teach people how to live. So they must try their best to obey the Sermon on the Mount. They must be loving and live the way Jesus said to live. Then, if they're *very* good and *very* obedient, they'll go to heaven. But if they don't do their best, they fail the test and go to hell.

This isn't true. Jesus *can* save you, and He *does* save you. He doesn't need your help. You don't need to be an extra-good Christian to go to heaven. It's not your own goodness that saves you. It's *Jesus'* goodness that does it. You just have to believe in Him and trust Him. Then He does everything that needs to be done to give you eternal life.

Of course, when you're a Christian, you will love God. You will obey Jesus and do what He said to do. But you obey Him because you *love* Him. And you love Him because He saved you, not because you're trying to save yourself. The apostle Paul said that it's only by God's mercy that you go to heaven. God had mercy on you when you didn't deserve it. You didn't earn God's mercy by being extra good.

Some sad people think they must *earn* their

salvation. They think it's like working at a job. If they do good deeds, God will pay them wages. The wages He will pay them is eternal life in heaven. But if that were true, they would earn their way into heaven by their *own* goodness. Then they could boast how good they were. But that simply doesn't happen.

You're saved by the grace of God. Grace is when someone has mercy on you when you don't deserve it. The apostle Paul said, "For it is by God's grace that you have been saved through faith. It is not the result of your own efforts, but God's gift, so that no one can boast about it" (Ephesians 2:8–9 GNT). He also said, "If God chose them by grace, then it is not for the things they have done. If they could be made God's people by what they did, then God's gift of grace would not really be a gift" (Romans 11:6 ICB).

The Bible says, "Abraham believed God, and because of his faith God accepted him as righteous" (Romans 4:3 GNT). God accepts you too. You just need to believe in Jesus.

Do you *help* Jesus save you by listening to how He tells you to live, and doing it?

God gave you eternal life as a gift. How does that make you feel?

22. WHAT DO ANGELS LOOK LIKE?

\\\\\\\\\\\\\\\\\\\\\\\

Angels look like people. That much we know for sure. But many people think there are male and female angels, that angels always dress in long white robes, have blond hair, huge white wings sticking out of their backs, and shiny halos floating above their heads. Almost all these ideas are wrong.

Every time the Bible describes angels, it says that they looked like men. Now, there *could* be female angels too. But if there are, the Bible doesn't talk about them. And there really doesn't need to be male and female angels, because they don't get married (Mark 12:25). Plus, they never die, so God doesn't need to keep creating more baby angels.

All those pictures you've seen of baby angels called "cherubs" and "cherubim" are false. There *are* cherubim, but they're not angels. The Bible talks about angels separately. The apostle John wrote, "I heard angels, thousands and millions of them! They stood around. . .the four living creatures [cherubim], and the elders" (Revelation 5:11 GNT). In Ezekiel, the prophet calls them "cherubim." They have faces like eagles, lions, bulls, and men. And they have six wings, eyes all over their bodies, and feet like a calf (See Ezekiel 1:5–14; Revelation 4:6–8 NKJV).

There are other creatures in heaven called seraphim. They have mostly human bodies, but have six wings, just like the cherubim (see Isaiah 6:2 NKJV).

Many people think angels have wings too. But if they did, they'd probably have *six* wings—like cherubim and seraphim—not just two. But whenever the Israelites met angels, the angels looked just like normal people. That means no wings. It also means that the angels had beards like regular men.

That's why people at first thought that they *were* just men (see Genesis 19:1–3; Judges 6:11–13; 13:3–21). If they'd had big wings, people would have noticed that immediately. But they looked normal—just very awesome. Samson's mother said, "A man of God came to me. He looked like an angel of God, very awesome" (Judges 13:6 NIV).

Angels don't usually let their full power and beauty shine when they're on earth. Most of the time, they look like regular people. Normally you only see how glorious they appear when you're in the spiritual world. "I looked up. And I saw a man. . . . His body was like shiny yellow quartz. His face was bright like lightning, and his eyes were like fire. His arms and legs were shiny like polished bronze" (Daniel 10:5–6 ICB).

What's the difference between angels and cherubim?

Do we know for sure that angels have two wings and halos?

23. WHAT DO ANGELS DO?

\\\\\\\\\\\\\\\\\\\\\\\\

You can't see angels. That means that, most of the time, you have no idea what they're doing. You might think they just stand there all day, watching you. But angels are very busy doing many things.

The Bible asks, "What are the angels, then? They are spirits who serve God and are sent by him to help those who are to receive salvation" (Hebrews 1:14 GNT). The first thing to know is that angels serve God. And they're here to help you. They don't stop helping you when you are saved. Angels keep helping you till you get to heaven.

The Hebrew word translated "angel" in the Bible is *malak*. It means "messenger." So you guessed it! One of the jobs angels do is carry messages from God to people on earth. For example, the angel Gabriel took a message to Zacharias, and later to Mary (Luke 1:8–13; 26–38).

Angels take care of you and give you strength. After Jesus had been in the desert forty days, the devil tempted Him. Then "angels came and took care of Jesus" (Matthew 4:11 NLT). And the same thing happened after Jesus prayed in the Garden of Gethsemane. "Then an angel from heaven appeared and strengthened him" (Luke 22:43 NLT).

Angels also protect people. The Bible says: "His angel guards those who honor the LORD and rescues them from danger" (Psalm 34:7 GNT). There are sometimes two or more angels taking care of you. "God will put his angels in charge of you to protect you wherever you go. They will hold you up with their hands to keep you from hurting your feet on the stones" (Psalm 91:11–12 GNT).

Another job they have is to fight evil angels called demons. The angel Gabriel told Daniel that he had fought against a powerful evil spirit called the Prince of Persia. Only the archangel Michael had helped him (see Daniel 9:21; 10:12–13, 20–21). Later, Michael and his angels fought a terrific battle against the devil and his angels in heaven (see Revelation 12:7–9).

Angels have fantastic powers. Twice when God's people were being attacked, angels struck the enemies blind (see Genesis 19:9–11; 2 Kings 6:15–18). When enemies threaten to kill you, God can wipe them out instead. One time, "an angel of the LORD went to the Assyrian camp and killed 185,000 soldiers" (Isaiah 37:36 GNT).

Your guardian angel has a big job. Make sure to thank God for him.

- -

Can you name three things that angels do?

Why do you usually not know what angels are doing?

24. WHY DO MY GUARDIAN ANGELS SOMETIMES NOT PROTECT ME?

\\\\\\\\\\\\\\\\\\\\\\\\\\\\\\

The Lord promised that He would put his angels in charge of you to protect you wherever you go. He promised they would even keep you from hurting your feet on stones. (See Psalm 91:11–12.) But sometimes, God's people still have accidents. Sometimes they get sick. Are their guardian angels forgetting to do their job? No. There are different reasons for this.

The main reason is that since Adam and Eve sinned, people then had accidents and illnesses. The Bible says, "People are born for trouble" (Job 5:7 NLT). Your guardian angels protect you from lots of accidents and trouble. So trouble passes by you and you never even knew it existed. You usually only notice the times when you *have* accidents and trouble.

You usually feel miserable when you're sick. But often God uses illness to do good things in your life. One believer told God, "Before I suffered, I did wrong. But now I obey your word" (Psalm 119:67 ICB). He added, "My suffering was good for me, for it taught me to pay attention to your decrees [commands]" (Psalm 119:71 NLT).

Suffering also forces you to pray and get close to God. And going through a lot of troubles teaches you patience.

Another reason is, "A man reaps what he sows" (Galatians 6:7 NIV). Whatever kind of seeds you plant, that's what will grow. If you get mad at your friends every time they visit you, they'll stop visiting. If you don't bother to brush your teeth, you get cavities. If you get in a panic, you can rush and cause an accident. If you're careless and don't look after your belongings, you lose them. This list goes on and on.

People bring much suffering upon themselves. But they then often expect God to fix all their problems—and fix them quickly. Then they blame Him if He doesn't. But you must honestly admit that you *caused* the problem, and ask God to forgive you. And often He wants *you* to take steps to fix it.

And finally, God usually only does miracles when you pray. He promises to do something when you pray with all your heart (Jeremiah 33:3). But often "you do not have because you do not ask" (James 4:2 NKJV). It can take real work to pray, and many people give up easily. But "be patient in trouble, and keep on praying" (Romans 12:12 NLT).

- -

What are some reasons your guardian angels don't protect you?

What does the saying, "You reap what you sow," mean?

25. WHY DID GOD MAKE THE DEVIL?

\\\\\\\\\\\\\\\\\\\\\\\\\\\\

Some people wonder why God created the devil, since God is good and the devil is evil. But remember, after God finished creating, "God saw everything that He had made, and indeed *it was* very good" (Genesis 1:31 NKJV). So was the devil "very good" in the beginning? Yes, he actually was. The devil was a cherub, one of the glorious cherubim. He was called Lucifer (Isaiah 14:12 KJV). In another translation, he was simply called "shining star" (NLT).

What do cherubim do? They guard God's throne. That's why the devil was called "a guardian cherub" (Ezekiel 28:14 NIV). Cherubim are closer to God than any other angel or creature. They sing songs of praise to God all the time (see Revelation 4:6–9). The devil once had a very important position. But he wasn't satisfied. He wanted to be worshipped like God.

God said: "You were in Eden, the garden of God; every precious stone adorned [covered] you . . . . You were anointed as a guardian cherub, for so I ordained you. You were on the holy mount of God; you walked among the fiery stones. You were blameless in your ways from the day you were created till wickedness was found in you" (Ezekiel 28:13–15 NIV).

What wickedness was found in the devil? Pride. He became proud. God said, "'How you are fallen from heaven, O shining star, son of the morning!'... For you said to yourself, 'I will ascend to heaven and set my throne above God's stars. I will preside [rule] on the mountain of the gods far away in the north. I will climb to the highest heavens and be like the Most High'" (Isaiah 14:12–14 NLT).

What happened next? Jesus said, "I saw Satan fall like lightning from heaven" (Luke 10:18 NIV). Yes. Jesus was there the day Satan and his angels fell. Some people think this *next* verse also describes Satan's fall: "The huge dragon was thrown out—that ancient serpent, named the Devil, or Satan, that deceived the whole world. He was thrown down to earth, and all his angels with him" (Revelation 12:9 GNT). But this verse happens at the end of time, when Satan attacks heaven—and is cast down.

God created all the fallen angels too. In the beginning, they were also "very good." But they listened to the devil's lies and joined him in his rebellion against God. When they fell with Satan, they became evil angels—in other words, demons.

Do people also sometimes start out good, and end up bad?

Why is pride such a terrible sin?

26. DOES THE DEVIL REALLY LOOK LIKE A DRAGON?

\\\\\\\\\\\\\\\\\\\\\\\\\\

The apostle John was taken up to heaven, where he had many visions. A vision is like having a dream when you're awake. In one of John's visions, he saw the devil attacking the church—God's people. He also saw the Archangel Michael and his angels fighting Satan and his evil angels. John wrote:

> "There was a huge red dragon with seven heads and ten horns and a crown on each of his heads. With his tail he dragged a third of the stars out of the sky and threw them down to the earth. . . . Then war broke out in heaven. Michael and his angels fought against the dragon, who fought back with his angels; but the dragon was defeated. . . . The huge dragon was thrown out—that ancient serpent, named the Devil, or Satan, that deceived the whole world. He was thrown down to earth, and all his angels with him."
>
> Then the dragon began to chase a woman. She had given birth to a baby boy. "And then from his mouth the dragon poured out a flood of water after the woman, so that it would carry her away" (Revelation 12:3–4, 7–9, 15 GNT).

People wonder, "Does the devil really look like a seven-headed dragon? Does a flood actually come out of his mouth?" No. God was giving John a vision. And the dragon didn't actually drag stars out of the sky. The stars symbolized angels.

In this same vision, John saw a pregnant woman "whose dress was the sun and who had the moon under her feet and a crown of twelve stars on her head" (v. 1). This woman is the church—God's people. But is the church actually a pregnant woman? Does she really wear the sun? No. God gave John a vision to show him important lessons.

The apostle John also had a vision of Jesus. And what did Jesus look like? John said, "I saw a Lamb that looked as if it had been slaughtered.... He had seven horns and seven eyes" (Revelation 5:6 NLT). Do you think that's what Jesus *actually* looks like? Of course not!

However, the devil can disguise himself and change his appearance. He sometimes changes himself to look like a good angel. "Even Satan disguises himself as an angel of light" (2 Corinthians 11:14 NLT). So the devil *can* change himself to look like a dragon for a while. But that's not how he normally looks.

- -

Does the devil normally look like a dragon?
  Why do you think that?

What is a vision? How are they like parables?

27. WHAT IS "SIN"?

\\\\\\\\\\\\\\\\\\\\\\\\\

Sin is anything you think, say, or do that dis-obeys God. If you lie, cheat, are greedy, hate people, hold a grudge, seek revenge, or take things without asking, you're sinning. God is love, and He does everything in love. He wants people to live lives of love too. Not just most of the time, but *all the time*. No one can do that, of course.

Everyone is a sinner. The Bible says, "For all have sinned and fall short of the glory of God" (Romans 3:23 NKJV). If you think you measure up to God's glory, you're only fooling yourself. Jesus was the only man who never sinned. He said, "I always do those things that please Him" (John 8:29 NKJV).

The New Testament was first written in Greek. And often the word translated as "sin" in your Bible is the Greek word *hamartia*. It means "to miss the mark." Every person on earth has missed the mark—in big ways or in small ways. Most people think sinful thoughts or do selfish things many times a day. And if they don't do anything bad for a whole day, they're proud of it. And pride is a sin.

The apostle James wrote: "This royal law is found in the Scriptures: 'Love your neighbor as you love yourself.' If you obey this law, then you are doing right. . . . A person might follow all of God's law. But if he fails to obey even one command, he is guilty of breaking all the commands in that law.

God said, 'You must not be guilty of adultery.' The same God also said, 'You must not murder anyone.' So if you do not take part in adultery, but you murder someone, then you are guilty of breaking all of God's law" (James 2:8, 10–11 ICB).

Here's how that applies to you: say you never steal even one little candy. You don't even take one cookie without asking—even if you're very hungry and your mom brings a fresh batch out of the oven. Your dad may even boast to people how honest you are. So you may think you're pretty good. But if you tease your sister or laugh when something bad happens to a bully, you're still sinning.

You may think, "I'm not a sinner. I don't rob banks or kill people." But you don't have to do horrible things that people talk about on TV to be a sinner. Some sins are very big. Other sins are small. But they're all sins. Every person on earth has fallen short and sinned. That's why everyone needs Jesus to save them.

What does the Greek word translated as *sin* actually mean?

Some people think they don't sin. Are they right?

28. IS IT A SIN TO GET MAD?

\\\\\\\\\\\\\\\\\\\\\\\\\\

You probably get mad from time to time. But hopefully, you don't get *so* mad that you slam doors, throw things, and hurt people. It's easy to see why that kind of anger is a sin. But you can also cause damage to people's emotions with your anger. Say you get mad easily. You let even little things make you furious. Or you get mad so often that people feel like they have to tiptoe around you. Or maybe you throw temper tantrums to get your way. The Bible warns against such anger, saying:

"People with a hot temper do foolish things; wiser people remain calm" (Proverbs 14:17 GNT). "People with quick tempers cause a lot of quarreling and trouble" (Proverbs 29:22 GNT). "Control your temper, for anger labels you a fool" (Ecclesiastes 7:9 NLT).

But even gentle people get angry at times. Not all anger is bad. After all, God created your emotions—love, joy, peace, sorrow, and even anger. Some people think that *all* anger is wrong. They even think Jesus sinned when He got angry. When a roomful of religious leaders were being hypocrites, "Jesus was angry as he looked around at them" (Mark 3:5 GNT). Once His disciples stopped small children from coming to Him. "When Jesus saw what was happening, he was angry with his disciples" (Mark 10:14 NLT).

Anger is not always wrong. Ephesians 4:26

(ICB) says, "When you are angry, do not sin." So you can be angry, but *not* be sinning. There are good reasons to get angry at times—like if you see a bully tormenting little kids.

The catch is, you shouldn't have a quick temper. "Always be willing to listen and slow to speak. Do not become angry easily" (James 1:19 ICB). God Himself gets angry at times, but the Bible says, "The Lord shows mercy and is kind. He does not become angry quickly, and he has great love" (Psalm 103:8 ICB).

And arguing isn't always wrong. Even godly men have different opinions, and argue. One time, Paul and Barnabas had a heated argument. Paul was the apostle who wrote 1 Corinthians 13, the Love Chapter. And the Bible says, "Barnabas was a good man, full of the Holy Spirit and full of faith" (Acts 11:24 ICB). But "their disagreement was so sharp that they separated" (Acts 15:39 NLT). Thankfully, they later worked out their differences and got along again.

Most of the time, pride and a quick temper are the main causes of arguments. So avoid them.

- -

People with quick tempers cause a lot of *what*?

Is anger always a sin?

29. IS IT OKAY TO TELL A LITTLE WHITE LIE?

\\\\\\\\\\\\\\\\\\\\\\\\

Many people lie all the time. They're in such a habit of telling lies that their first reaction is to lie. If you ask them a question they don't want to answer, they'll lie. If they wreck something, they'll lie and say they didn't do it. If they took something without asking, they'll lie about that too.

When you tell them that lying hurts people, they have trouble believing you. For them, lies are helpful things. Lies help them get out of bad situations. Lies keep them from getting embarrassed. Lies save them money. Lies help them avoid punishment. They can't imagine a day without telling lies.

But the Bible is not fond of lies. It commands, "Do not steal or cheat or lie" (Leviticus 19:11 GNT). And the apostle Paul said, "So you must stop telling lies. Tell each other the truth" (Ephesians 4:25 ICB).

You may say, "Okay. I understand that big lies, lies that hurt people, are bad. But is it okay to tell a little white lie?" But remember, for many people, almost all lies are "little white lies." Because lies help them, they think they're good.

Your "old self" is who you were before Jesus saved you. But you have a new life now. So put off the old, selfish ways, hurting people, and lying.

"Do not lie to one another, for you have put off the old self with its habits" (Colossians 3:9 GNT).

You should always speak the truth. On the other hand, you must avoid hurting others. Don't just bluntly give your opinion without thinking about people's feelings. Paul said, "We will speak the truth with love" (Ephesians 4:15 ICB). If your little sister asks what you think of her drawing, and you think it's a mess, don't say that. Look at her picture again and think of something nice to say about it. Maybe she used lots of colors. So you could tell her, "It's very colorful." Don't lie. But do consider other people's feelings.

Also, don't deceive people. To deceive someone is to make them think something that isn't true. For example, let's say you went to your older brother's room and broke something. Later, he calls you to his room and asks if you broke it. You might be clever and say, "I just came to your room now." You're not lying, but you're trying to make him believe a lie. So don't deceive people either.

Why should you not tell even "little white lies"?

How is deceiving people a lot like telling them a lie?

30. WHY IS IT WRONG TO SWEAR OR TELL DIRTY JOKES?

\\\\\\\\\\\\\\\\\\\\\\\\\

The Bible says, "Don't use foul or abusive language. Let everything you say be good and helpful, so that your words will be an encouragement to those who hear them" (Ephesians 4:29 NLT). What does "Don't use foul language" mean? Well, first of all, what does "foul" mean? Foul means a bad or rotten smell, like a baby's messy diaper. That's what foul language sounds like.

The apostle Paul wrote, "Also, there must be no evil talk among you. You must not speak foolishly or tell evil jokes. These things are not right for you." (Ephesians 5:4 ICB). It's all right to have fun and tell jokes, but don't get all foolish. Have you ever seen some kid go completely bananas? He starts off saying a few silly things and acting mindless to get people to laugh. But soon he's saying every crazy thought that comes into his head. Then nobody's laughing any more—except *other* foolish kids.

And the thing about kids who try too hard to get people to laugh is that often they start insulting other people. They say hurtful things about their friends to get people to laugh. You're not supposed to hurt people with humor. So watch what you say.

Paul wrote, "But now is the time to get rid of anger, rage, malicious [evil] behavior, slander, and dirty language" (Colossians 3:8 NLT). Instead of using dirty language, you are supposed to get *rid* of it. Say there's a messy baby diaper in your house. Your mom doesn't leave it laying around, making the house stinky. She drops it in the garbage and gets rid of it. Then the garbage men take it away.

Some grown-ups say, "Kids shouldn't swear." But the Bible says adults shouldn't swear either. So why *do* kids swear? Often it's because they hear their parents doing it. Or it's because they hear other kids swear. And they want to be accepted by their friends. The "tough" kids in the group swear, so other kids feel like it's cool. And they want to fit in. So they use foul language too.

These days, people say someone is swearing or cursing if they use dirty language. But there used to be a difference between curse words and potty humor. Originally, to use "curse words" meant to ask God to judge someone and send them to hell. That wasn't dirty, but it was hateful and mean. The Bible says, "Don't curse them; pray that God will bless them" (Romans 12:14 NLT).

Why do some kids swear?

What should you do instead of using curse words?

31. ARE GHOSTS AND HAUNTED HOUSES REAL?

\\\\\\\\\\\\\\\\\\\\\\\\\\\\\\

Christians believe that when people die, they go to heaven or to a place of punishment. But some people who aren't Christians believe that after people die, their spirits can stick around for years. They think they become ghosts and haunt places they once lived. They believe they make noises, and even appear.

Are ghosts real? Yes, they are. The ancient Jews believed that after a person died, their spirit sometimes stuck around for three days. Bible people sometimes thought they saw these spirits. When Jesus' disciples were in a boat on the Sea of Galilee, they saw a man walking on the waves. They cried out, "It's a ghost!" (Matthew 14:26 NLT). They were sure it was a ghost because no man could walk on water. But it was Jesus.

After Jesus was crucified, His disciples knew He was dead. So they were shocked when He appeared to them. "Suddenly the Lord himself stood among them and said to them, 'Peace be with you.' They were terrified, thinking that they were seeing a ghost. But he said to them. . .'Look at my hands and my feet, and see that it is I myself. Feel me, and you will know, for a ghost doesn't have flesh and bones, as you can see I have'" (Luke 24:36–39 GNT).

One of Job's friends, Eliphaz, may have seen a real ghost. Then again, maybe he *didn't*. Eliphaz said, "I could see something standing there; I stared, but couldn't tell what it was" (Job 4:16 GNT). What was this spirit? An angel or a ghost? We don't know. But it talked to Eliphaz about angels (v. 18).

Most people who think they're seeing or hearing a ghost actually aren't. People who go to haunted houses say they can "feel" a ghost there. But much of the time, it's just their imagination playing tricks on them. If there really was a spirit there, it was most likely a demon. Good angels can change their appearance to make you think they're people. And demons (evil angels) can do the same (Hebrews 13:2; 2 Corinthians 11:14). So stay away from such places.

If your loved ones were believers, they went to heaven when they died. Their spirit usually *can't* come back to earth to visit you. So don't try to contact them. You'll go to heaven one day and see them again.

And don't worry about ghosts. God puts his mighty angels around you. If you stay close to God, His angels will protect you from *all* evil spirits.

- -

Are ghosts real?

Are people usually seeing a ghost when they *think* they're seeing one?

32. WHY IS IT WRONG TO GO TO A MEDIUM OR A FORTUNETELLER?

\\\\\\\\\\\\\\\\\\\\\\\\

You might see a sign at a state fair: PSYCHIC READINGS BY MADAME ZOLA. What if she stood in her doorway and said, "Hey! Come here. I'll tell your fortune for free." What should you do? Or what if your grandma died, and a medium promised she could talk to her spirit? What if she said she'd give you a message from your grandma? What should you do?

You should quickly leave. Have nothing to do with fortunetellers or palm-readers or mediums. There once was a wicked king named Manasseh. The Bible says, "He practiced divination and magic and consulted fortunetellers and mediums. He sinned greatly against the LORD and stirred up his anger" (2 Chronicles 33:6 GNT).

The prophet Isaiah said, "But people will tell you to ask for messages from fortunetellers and mediums.... They will say, 'After all, people should ask for messages from the spirits and consult the dead on behalf of the living.' You are to answer them, 'Listen to what the LORD is teaching you! Don't listen to mediums'" (Isaiah 8:19–20 GNT).

Now, most mediums and fortunetellers are fakes. They have no power at all. They only pretend to know your future. They only pretend to contact the spirits of the dead. But some of them have *real* power. But that doesn't mean they're helpful. They're dangerous. In olden days, the law said: "Men and women among you who act as mediums or who consult the spirits of the dead must be put to death" (Leviticus 20:27 NLT).

Why were they so dangerous? Because they made God's people *defiled* (filthy and dirty) in the spirit. Moses warned, "Do not defile yourselves by turning to mediums or to those who consult the spirits of the dead" (Leviticus 19:31 NLT). To "consult" someone means to ask them questions. How did they make people filthy? It's because they got their power from the devil.

Once a fortuneteller followed Paul and Silas around, bothering them. So they cast the evil spirit out of her, and she could no longer tell fortunes. Luke wrote: "We met a slave girl who had a spirit that enabled her to tell the future. She earned a lot of money for her masters by telling fortunes." Paul "said to the demon within her, 'I command you in the name of Jesus Christ to come out of her.' And instantly it left her" (Acts 16:16, 18 NLT).

- -

Why does the Bible warn you against mediums and fortunetellers?

Do some mediums or fortunetellers have real power? Where is it from?

33. WHAT'S WRONG WITH ASTROLOGY?

\\\\\\\\\\\\\\\\\\\\\\\\\\\\

Ancient peoples looked for messages in the stars. They named some groups of stars (constellations) after people and animals. Astrologers divided the heavens into twelve constellations. These were Aries, Taurus, Gemini, Cancer, Leo, Virgo, Libra, Scorpio, Sagittarius, Capricorn, Aquarius, and Pisces. If someone was born when the sun was in the constellation Scorpio, astrologers said, "You're a Scorpio."

Astrologers noticed that five stars moved across the heavens. These "stars" were planets, but the ancients thought they moved because they were gods. So they named them Mercury, Venus, Mars, Jupiter, and Saturn. And they worshipped them.

Astrologers decided that each "god" ruled *two* constellations, and the sun god and moon god each ruled *one* constellation. For example, they said Mars ruled Aries and Scorpio. So as Mars moved across the sky, astrologers believed it made things happen on earth. One day it brought people happiness. A couple days later, Mars was in a different part of the heavens. Then it brought them problems.

Astrologers also decided that Jupiter ruled Sagittarius and Pisces, and Saturn ruled Capricorn and Aquarius. But in 1781, the planet Uranus was discovered. Astrologers announced that Uranus was the *true* ruler of Aquarius. They said, "Saturn doesn't rule Aquarius, after all. Our bad.

Forget everything we said for thousands of years about Aquarius."

In 1846, the planet Neptune was discovered. Astrologers decided that it was the *true* ruler of Pisces. They said, "Jupiter doesn't rule Pisces, after all. Neptune does."

In 1930, Pluto was discovered. Astrologers decided that Pluto was the *true* ruler of Scorpio. They said, "Mars doesn't rule Scorpio, after all. Pluto does." How ridiculous! Will they *please* make up their minds!

The Bible warns, "Do not act like the other nations, who try to read their future in the stars. Do not be afraid of their predictions" (Jeremiah 10:2 NLT). God said, "I make fools of fortunetellers and frustrate the predictions of astrologers. . . I. . .show that their wisdom is foolishness" (Isaiah 44:25 GNT).

Many Israelites believed in astrology, so God mocked them. He said, "Let your astrologers come forward and save you—those people who study the stars, who map out the zones of the heavens and tell you from month to month what is going to happen to you" (Isaiah 47:13 GNT). But the astrologers couldn't help.

Astrology may seem like harmless fun. But it's based on pagan gods and is foolish. Don't waste time with it.

What would you say if someone asks what sign you are?

Can you name one foolish thing about astrology?

34. DIDN'T THE WISE MEN LEARN ABOUT JESUS' BIRTH THROUGH ASTROLOGY?

\\\\\\\\\\\\\\\\\\\\\\\

Matthew tells us that wise men came from the East after Jesus was born. Matthew used the Greek word *magi*. The magi were Persian wise men or priests from the Parthian Empire. The magi were usually also astrologers. One night they saw a bright star in the sky in the direction of Israel (see Matthew 2:1–2). They knew that something very important was happening.

People have different guesses about what the star was. Some think it was a comet. Others guess that a supernova appeared. (A supernova is when a star explodes and gets very big and bright for a short time.) Others say that a bright "star" formed when two planets, Jupiter and Saturn, passed very close to each other.

God could have used one of these natural things. But remember the unusual things the star did. When the wise men left Jerusalem, "the star which they had seen in the East went before them, till it came and stood over where the young Child was" (Matthew 2:9 NKJV). The star "went before them" as they rode five miles to Bethlehem then "stood over" the exact house where Jesus was. It couldn't have been millions of miles away in space or it would have appeared over Jerusalem as much as over Bethlehem.

The magi could have been looking for astrological signs, however, God did a special miracle to get their attention.

Some people argue that these magi must have seen a planet in a certain constellation. Then they used astrology to figure out that a great king had been born in Israel. But remember: for centuries before this, God *mocked* astrology. He warned people to pay *no attention* to it (see Isaiah 47:13; Jeremiah 10:2). Why would God say, "Pay no attention to astrology" for hundreds of years—then suddenly say, "Pay attention to it now"? It makes no sense.

Here's what most likely happened: at that time there were hundreds of thousands of Jews living in Parthia. Among those Jews were many wise Jewish scribes. And they all knew this prophecy: "I look into the future, and I see the nation of Israel. A king, like a bright star, will arise in that nation" (Numbers 24:17 GNT). After the Persian wise men saw the star over Israel, they could have asked Jewish wise men about it. Then the Jewish wise men could have told them what it meant. The King of the Jews had been born.

- -

What do you think the "star" was that the wise men saw?

How did the magi know that a great king had been born in Israel?

35. WHY IS SEVEN GOD'S NUMBER AND NOT THIRTEEN?

\\\\\\\\\\\\\\\\\\\\\\

The Bible doesn't *say* that seven is God's number. People get that idea because there are sometimes seven good things in God's Word. For example, after creating the heavens and the earth, God rested on the seventh day. A prophet saw a stone with seven eyes in it. There are seven spirits before God's throne. The Lamb that symbolizes Jesus has seven horns and seven eyes (Genesis 2:2; Zechariah 3:9; Revelation 1:4; 5:6).

But wait! There were sometimes seven *bad* things. For example, the seven sons of Sceva were beaten up by a man with an evil spirit. The dragon that symbolizes the devil has seven heads (Acts 19:13–16; Revelation 12:3).

Many people also believe that the number thirteen brings bad luck. They think Friday the thirteenth is a very unlucky day. We don't know why people started to think this. Some say it's because when Jesus and His twelve disciples ate the Last Supper, there were thirteen people at the table—and the thirteenth person, Judas, betrayed Jesus. But that's only a guess. But in Italy and some other countries, people think that thirteen is a "lucky" number.

Many Chinese people think that four is a very unlucky number. They won't buy a house if it has a four in its address. This is because the Chinese word for "four" sounds like the word for "death."

People who think some numbers are lucky and others unlucky are superstitious. They often think many strange things too. For example, they may be afraid to step on a crack in the sidewalk. They think it will bring them "bad luck." Or they may think that they'll be jinxed (cursed) if a black cat crosses their path. They may keep a "lucky penny" in their pocket. They may hang a rabbit's foot in their car to protect them. All these things are nonsense.

Some people get worried when they hear about something bad happening. They don't want it to happen to *them*. So they quickly say, "Knock on wood!" Then they look for some wood to knock on. Why do they do such a silly thing? Long ago, people believed spirits lived inside trees. People worshipped them. So they may have knocked on the tree to wake up the spirit. Then they asked it to do them a favor or protect them. Don't do that.

You shouldn't be afraid of "bad luck." If you believe in Jesus, God is in your life. He will bless you and protect you from evil.

Does seven *always* stand for good things in the Bible?

What other kinds of things do superstitious people believe?

36. IS REINCARNATION REAL?

\\\\\\\\\\\\\\\\\\\\\\\\\\

Sometimes you might see a TV program where a woman says, "In a past life, I was Pocahontas, the Indian Princess. After I died, I was born as a baby in France. I grew up and became Queen Marie Antoinette. I had curly hair and ate lots of cake." What on earth is she talking about? She's talking about reincarnation.

Reincarnation means "to come in a body again." People who believe this think that after they die, their soul goes into the spiritual world for a while. Then it comes back to earth as a new baby, and lives another life. They claim that people do this over and over and over again. Ideas about reincarnation come mostly from the Hindu religion of India. Hindus also worship many gods and goddesses.

Many Hindus think if they live a good life, they'll be born as a rich person in their next life. Or they may be born as a wonderful being in a heavenly kingdom. But if they live a bad life, they may be born next time as a beggar. Or as a rat or a cockroach. Or worse yet, they'll be born in hell. There they'll suffer for many years until they die.

Hindus think if they learn from past mistakes, they'll live better and better lives. Finally, they'll be perfect and won't keep being born. Then they'll be happy forever. But millions and millions of Hindus have become unhappy with their religion.

So they put their faith in Jesus and became Christians. They once believed in reincarnation, but they don't anymore. So why should *you* believe it?

The fact is reincarnation is wrong. The Bible says, "Everyone must die once, and after that be judged by God" (Hebrews 9:27 GNT). Every person on earth will "die *once*." Then after they die, God will judge them for how they lived their life—their *one* life.

Many people don't like the idea of God judging them after they die. The Roman Governor Felix didn't. Paul was telling Felix about Jesus. "But as Paul went on discussing about goodness, self-control, and the coming Day of Judgment, Felix was afraid and said, 'You may leave now'" (Acts 24:25 GNT).

People prefer to believe in reincarnation. They think that God doesn't judge them. They just keep being born in new lives. They learn all by themselves to be better and better people. They think they get hundreds of chances to live good lives. But that's not true. People only get to live *one* life.

Why do many people believe in reincarnation?

Do people really live many lives? Why do you think that?

37. WHY IS IT BAD TO SMOKE CIGARETTES?

\\\\\\\\\\\\\\\\\\\\\\\\\\\\

Smoking cigarettes is bad because it can ruin your health and even kill you. Cigarette smoke has many harmful chemicals in it. Nearly seventy of these chemicals cause cancer, and many others are poisonous. Here are just a few of the chemicals in cigarettes. This list shows what these chemicals are *also* used for:

Acetone is found in nail polish remover. Acetic acid is a chemical in hair dye. Arsenic is used in rat poison. Butane is used in lighter fluid. Cadmium is found in battery acid. Carbon monoxide is in car exhaust fumes. Lead is a poison used in batteries. Methanol is used in rocket fuel. Nicotine is used to kill insects. Tar is used for paving roads. Toluene is used to make paint.

Paul wrote: "Don't you realize that your body is the temple of the Holy Spirit, who lives in you and was given to you by God? You do not belong to yourself, for God bought you with a high price. So you must honor God with your body" (1 Corinthians 6:19–20 NLT). How do you honor God with your body? One way is by taking care of it and not harming it.

Even too "good things" like sugar and chocolate can be bad for you if you eat too much of them. Sugar causes tooth decay, so always brush your teeth after eating candy. Even soft drinks (also called soda or pop) can cause tooth decay, so rinse your mouth out after drinking some.

Many Christians also believe that it's wrong to drink alcohol. However, people in the Bible times often drank wine (Psalm 104:14–15 NLT). So some churches see nothing wrong with drinking alcohol—as long as people don't drink too much. But the problem is that *many* people drink too much. Once they start, they can't stop until they're so drunk they fall to the floor.

Alcohol causes terrible problems. Many people waste a lot of money on alcohol. Sometimes they don't have cash left over to buy food or pay their rent. They often drive their car when they're drunk. This can cause horrible accidents. And when they get drunk, they say and do bad things. The Bible says, "Do not get drunk with wine, which will only ruin you; instead, be filled with the Spirit" (Ephesians 5:18 GNT).

And drugs are very harmful. They can wreck your mind so that you can't think straight any more. People probably aren't going to try to give you illegal drugs yet, but they might as you get older. So make up your mind now to say no.

Why is it harmful to smoke cigarettes?

What kind of problems can drinking alcohol cause?

38. COULD GOD HAVE REALLY CREATED THE WORLD IN JUST SIX DAYS?

\\\\\\\\\\\\\\\\\\\\\\\\\\\

Yes, He could have. Jeremiah said to God, "You made the heavens and earth by your strong hand and powerful arm. Nothing is too hard for you!" (Jeremiah 32:17 NLT). In fact, God could have created the entire universe in six *seconds*. But God enjoyed creating so much that He stretched it out to make it last.

Christians have different ideas about the creation of the world. Those who believe that the days of Creation in Genesis were only 24 hours long, say that the earth is only 6,000 to 10,000 years old. Since they believe that the earth is young, they're called Young Earth Creationists.

Other Christians say that God created the world 4.5 billion years ago. Since they believe that the earth is very old, they're called Old Earth Creationists. They say that the "days" of creation were six different ages. Each age lasted many millions of years, and God was busy creating in each age.

Many people today don't believe in God. They don't think He created the earth and all life on it. They say everything happened by chance, and that evolution caused life to happen. But Christians who believe in Intelligent Design point out that evolution can't work by itself. These Christians say that God used evolution to create life, but that He guided it in every detail.

All of these Christians honor God and believe that He created the world and all life on it. But they have different ways to explain how He did it.

Here is one of the greatest proofs that God created life; scientists have found that the way life works is very similar to computer codes. Everywhere they look, these codes make life happen. DNA is written in code. It looks like it was created by a computer genius.

Now, when you see a computer code, you know that an intelligent person thought it up. If you told your friends that an awesome new computer game invented itself, they would laugh at you. None of them would believe you. Just so, when you see the amazing codes that make life work, you know that an intelligent Being invented that code. Life shows that a super-smart Person created it. That Person is God.

Also, the universe seems to be fine-tuned to support life. If the laws of science were only a *little* bit different, life couldn't exist. But it does! This is proof the God made the laws that run the universe.

Which way do you think God created the earth and life on it?

Why do you believe that an intelligent Being made nature?

39. WHY DID GOD REST ON THE SEVENTH DAY?

\\\\\\\\\\\\\\\\\\\\\\\\\\\\

God didn't rest because He was tired and needed to sleep. When the Bible says He rested, it means He stopped His work of creating. He had done enough. Then He sat back and enjoyed everything He had created. The Lord didn't get tired. The Bible says, "The LORD is the everlasting God, the Creator of all the earth. He never grows weak or weary" (Isaiah 40:28 NLT).

But God knew that people *do* get tired after a week of work. They need a rest. You get tired after a week of schoolwork. You need a break. So because even He rested from His work, God commanded His people to rest once a week also. But some people work all week, then work on the weekend too. They do this week after week. But after a while, it catches up with them. Don't overwork! You need to take off one day a week.

God said in the Ten Commandments: "Remember to keep the Sabbath as a holy day. You may work and get everything done during six days each week. But the seventh day is a day of rest to honor the Lord your God. On that day no one may do any work" (Exodus 20:8–10 ICB). The Jews call this day of rest the Sabbath. The Sabbath is Saturday. But most Christians rest on Sunday, because that was the day God raised Jesus from the dead.

The Pharisees took the command to "not do any work" too far. On the Sabbath, they wouldn't even allow people to *spit*. They said even that was work. Your spit might move some dirt, and that would be "plowing." They wouldn't even allow people to help someone who really needed help. But Jesus had mercy, and often healed people on that day. When the Pharisees criticized Him for "working," Jesus said, "My Father never stops working. And so I work, too" (John 5:17 ICB).

God created the universe in six days. That amazing work is all done. But God is still doing miracles large and small—even on Saturday and Sunday. Sometimes you *too* may need to do some emergency work then. But, for the most part, be sure to rest on the Sabbath. Or relax on Sunday. Take one day a week off from your work to honor God and to think about Him.

"Rest in the LORD" (Psalm 37:7 NKJV). Trust that He will take care of things while you're resting. Trust that He will supply all your needs.

What day does your family rest every week? Why?

What do you do to honor God on that day?

40. WHY DID GOD MAKE GERMS?

\\\\\\\\\\\\\\\\\\\\\\\\\\\

Bacteria and viruses are the two main kinds of germs in the world. We know that germs cause many, many kinds of illnesses. We also know that God created everything. So the question is, Why did He create germs?

Bacteria cause diseases like sore throats. They also cause leprosy and the Bubonic Plague. The Bubonic Plague killed millions of people from 1338–1351. That was awful! No wonder many people think *all* bacteria are bad. But most bacteria are harmless, and many do great good. Billions of good bacteria live in your body. There are about 500 different kinds of them. Many of them produce vitamins your body needs. Or they help you digest food. You couldn't survive without them.

Then why do *other* bacteria cause disease and death? It wasn't this way when the world was created. When God first created things, "God looked at everything he had made, and it was very good" (Genesis 1:31 icb). But Adam and Eve brought a curse on the earth. God said, "Since you...ate from the tree whose fruit I commanded you not to eat, the ground is cursed because of you" (Genesis 3:17 nlt). This was when some bacteria became harmful. What about viruses? They cause sicknesses such as influenza, dengue fever, and other deadly diseases. Viruses cause much evil and almost zero good. So God probably didn't create viruses in the beginning. They probably started out as good bacteria or good plasmids (pieces of DNA). Then they became deformed during the curse.

God told Adam and Eve that the ground was cursed. Paul explained that "all creation was subjected to God's curse." He said that "the creation looks forward to. . .freedom from death and decay" (Romans 8:20–21 NLT). Then the Kingdom of God will be on earth. There will be no more viruses.

Until that day, there are things Christians can do to help others. Mosquitoes give malaria to millions of people. Malaria kills over seven hundred thousand people every year. Yet, malaria can be cured. There are medicines for it. But often poor people can't afford the medicines. Christians can help them by donating money.

Cholera is a sickness caused by unclean water that gets into food. Nearly five million people get sick from cholera every year, and twenty thousand die. This is why Christian workers dig wells for poor villages. This is why doctors travel around, telling people how to avoid cholera. Love is God's answer to the suffering world.

Since germs cause sicknesses, why did God create them?

How can you help people who are suffering from diseases?

41. DOES THE BIBLE ACTUALLY TALK ABOUT DINOSAURS?

\\\\\\\\\\\\\\\\\\\\\\\\\\\\

Many Christians believe the Bible does indeed talk about dinosaurs. It says, "Look at Behemoth. . . . He eats grass like an ox. Look at the strength he has in his body. The muscles of his stomach are powerful! His tail extends like a cedar tree. The muscles of his thighs are woven together. His bones are like tubes of bronze metal. His legs are like bars of iron. . . . The hills, where the wild animals play, provide food for him" (Job 40:15–18, 20 icb).

Some people say this is talking about an elephant, but the Bible says, "His tail extends like a cedar tree." Have you ever seen an elephant's tail? It's as puny as a rope! But some dinosaurs' tails *were* thick like cedar trees. And think of this: "His bones are like tubes of bronze metal. His legs are like bars of iron." This sounds like an Argentinosaurus. That monster was over one hundred feet long and weighed one hundred tons. (That's as much as thirty-five elephants!) It was super-heavy. It *needed* legs like bars made of iron just to stand up.

And here's another monster. Psalms says, "See the ships sailing along, and Leviathan, which you made to play in the sea" (Psalm 104:26 NLT). Some Christians claim that Leviathan in Job 41 was a gigantic Plesiosaur of some kind. They grew up to thirty-four feet long. Most of their graceful body was made up of their very long neck.

The Bible says, "I will not fail to speak of Leviathan's limbs, its strength and its graceful form. Who can strip off its outer coat? Who can penetrate its double coat of armor? Who dares open the doors of its mouth, ringed about with fearsome teeth? Its back has rows of shields tightly sealed together" (Job 41:12–15 NIV).

Some people think the Bible was just talking about the Nile crocodile. But you don't usually think of "graceful form" when you think of crocodiles.

And think about this: "Smoke pours from its nostrils. . .flames dart from its mouth" (vv. 20–21). This probably started the legends of fire-breathing dragons. In fact, Leviathan may *not* have been a plesiosaur, after all. Maybe it was some amazing monster whose bones we haven't dug up yet. Very likely, there really *were* dragons! They just couldn't fly, that's all.

What do you think the verses about Behemoth describe? Why?

What do you think the verses about Leviathan describe? Why?

42. HOW DID EATING ONE APPLE CAUSE SO MANY PROBLEMS?

\\\\\\\\\\\\\\\\\\\\\\\\\\\\

The Bible says, "The LORD God placed the man in the Garden of Eden to tend and watch over it. But the LORD God warned him, 'You may freely eat the fruit of every tree in the garden—except the tree of the knowledge of good and evil. If you eat its fruit, you are sure to die'" (Genesis 2:15–17 NLT).

What was the forbidden fruit? Many people think it was an apple. But the Bible doesn't say that. We don't know what kind of fruit it was. It was probably some unusual fruit we've never seen. So why do people think it was an apple?

Well, the ancient Greeks heard the Bible story of the Garden of Eden. Then a Greek poet named Stesichorus made up his own story. He wrote a poem about an island far away that had a tree with golden apples. A group of women called Hesperides took care of the tree. And a serpent like a dragon guarded it. In his poem, Stesichorus said that if someone ate an apple, he would live forever.

You can see that Stesichorus had heard the Bible story about the Garden of Eden. He got his facts all mixed up. But this is where people get the idea that the forbidden fruit was an apple.

But how did the forbidden fruit—whatever it

was—cause so many problems? Well, think about this: Adam and Eve swallowed several mouthfuls of the fruit. Some people have a bad reaction when they eat even a little bit of certain fruit. Only one bite of a kiwi fruit and they get a rash on their body. One bite of a banana and they can barely breathe. Some people die if they eat even *one peanut*. Some chili peppers are so hot they burn your stomach. You have to rush to a hospital. The damage can last the rest of your life.

The forbidden fruit caused great damage to Adam and Eve's bodies. Their bodies started dying that very moment. The damage hurt them in many ways, and it lasted all their lives. And it affected everyone on earth who was born from them. The forbidden fruit even changed the way their brains thought. It probably changed the DNA in every cell in their body. That was one *very* dangerous fruit. No wonder God commanded them not to eat it.

- -

Do you think the forbidden fruit was an apple? Why do you think that?

How could the forbidden fruit change Adam and Eve and all their children?

43. WHY DO PEOPLE GET OLD AND DIE?

\\\\\\\\\\\\\\\\\\\\\\\\

In the beginning, God planned for people's bodies to live forever. He warned Adam, "You may eat the fruit from any tree in the garden. But you must not eat the fruit from the tree which gives the knowledge of good and evil. If you ever eat fruit from that tree, you will die!" (Genesis 2:16–17 ICB). At that time, Adam and Eve had eternal life. But God warned that they'd *lose* it if they disobeyed. And that's what happened. Adam and Eve ate the fruit and immediately their bodies lost the power to live forever. They started to die.

But they could have gotten eternal life back. They could have eaten from the Tree of Life. That's why God said, "We must keep him from eating some of the fruit from the tree of life. If he does, he will live forever" (Genesis 3:22 ICB). So the Lord sent Adam and Eve out of the Garden of Eden.

The human body is always making new cells to take the place of old cells. The DNA inside people's cells has all the information it needs to make perfect copies. But our cells *don't* keep producing perfect new cells forever. After a while when the cells are copying the information in the DNA, they make mistakes.

These mistakes are very tiny at first, and make

little difference. But after several years, the cells have made *many* mistakes, and these mistakes add up. They start causing serious changes. Important information that the body needs to make healthy cells is now missing or wrong. After a few years, there is *so* much damage that the cells don't work well anymore. Then, important organs like the heart, the liver, and the brain no longer work. In the end, the person's body dies.

Scientists have been looking for ways to help cells keep making copies without mistakes. They think it might one day be possible to stop bodies from aging. Then people will live hundreds of years again—even thousands of years.

But it might not be *so* easy to fix the problem. After all, sin caused the cells to start making mistakes. So sin causes people's bodies to age and die. If scientists *really* wanted to fix the problem, they would need to deal with the problem of sin. But they can't. Only Jesus Christ is able to wash away people's sins. And one day He will give His followers powerful, new eternal bodies.

What causes the body to age and eventually die?

How can people fix the problem and once again live forever?

44. HOW DID PEOPLE IN ANCIENT TIMES LIVE TO BE SO OLD?

\\\\\\\\\\\\\\\\\\\\\\\

Some people are very surprised when they read in the Bible that people used to live for hundreds of years. In fact, they lived nearly one thousand years!

Did people actually live that long? Yes. Remember, in the beginning, God made people to live *forever*. But when their bodies were damaged by sin, their cells began making mistakes when copying DNA. They still lived hundreds of years, and that's a long time. But it's not as long as *forever*.

Before the Flood, "Adam lived a total of 930 years. Then he died" (Genesis 5:5 ICB). "Seth lived a total of 912 years. Then he died" (v. 8). "Enosh lived a total of 905 years. Then he died" (v. 11). "Kenan lived a total of 910 years. Then he died" (v. 14). "Mahalalel lived a total of 895 years. Then he died" (v. 17). "Jared lived a total of 962 years. Then he died" (v. 20). "Methuselah lived a total of 969 years. Then he died" (v. 27).

After the Flood, however, people suddenly began living much shorter lives. Shem lived 600 years; Arphaxad lived 438 years; Peleg lived 239 years; Terah lived 205 years; Abraham lived 175 years, Jacob lived 147 years, Joseph lived 110 years; etc. (Genesis

11:10–26, 32; 25:7; 47:28; 50:26).

Jacob noticed how short people's lives were getting. When he first arrived in Egypt, Pharaoh asked him, "How old are you?" Jacob replied, "I have traveled this earth for 130 hard years. But my life has been short compared to the lives of my ancestors" (Genesis 47:8–9 NLT).

By Moses' day, lives were even shorter. He wrote, "Seventy years is all we have—eighty years, if we are strong; yet all they bring us is trouble and sorrow; life is soon over, and we are gone" (Psalm 90:10 GNT). These days, many nations have good food and healthcare, but most people still live only 70–80 years. A few people live to be 90 or even 100, but not many.

Why was there such a sudden, sharp drop in how long people lived after the Flood? Many Christians believe that before the Flood, mankind's DNA wasn't badly damaged by sin yet. Also, the earth's magnetic field was stronger. It protected the Earth from most harmful radiation. But after the Flood, this protection was weaker. So damage began building up quickly in people's DNA. And their lives began to be shorter.

- -

Why did people's lives become so much shorter after the Flood?

Why did Jacob think he'd had a short life when he was 130 years old?

45. HOW COULD SO MANY ANIMALS FIT ON NOAH'S ARK?

\\\\\\\\\\\\\\\\\\\\\\\\

Some little kids' picture books show the ark as a curvy boat, just big enough for a couple elephants, a pair of monkeys, one giraffe, and...that's about it. But the ark was huge! Hundreds and hundreds of elephants could have fit inside it!

God told Noah to make the ark, "450 feet long, 75 feet wide, and 45 feet high" (Genesis 6:15 GNT). The ark wasn't shaped like a modern ship. It was built like a huge, huge wooden box. It wasn't built to look beautiful.

Now, the ark was 45 feet high. So perhaps the lowest level, where the biggest animals were, had a ceiling 25 feet high. Then the two upper levels were each only 10 feet high. After all, the small animals didn't need high ceilings.

Okay, so we know the exact size of the ark. And Genesis 7:19–20 (NLT) tells us that when the ark was fully loaded, it sank 22 ½ feet deep in the sea. So half of the ark was under the water and half was above. And with these facts we can figure out how much the ark weighed.

The part of a ship underwater displaces water (pushes it out of the way). A ship always weighs exactly as much as the water it displaces. So when we multiply the ark's length and width by 22½ feet, we can figure out its weight. So let's do it. Okay, 450 feet x 75 feet x 22½ feet = 759,375 cubic feet.

One cubic foot of ocean water weighs around 62.4 pounds. So we know that the ark weighed 47,385,000 pounds. That's about 24,000 tons! (Read the book, *Noah's Ark for Kids* for more amazing information.)

Experts say that the wooden ark and the food and drinking water on it made up 90 percent of this weight. The animals weighed the other 10 percent. So let's divide 47,385,000 pounds by 10. We see that there were 4,738,500 pounds (2,400 tons) of animals. Now, the average animal is as big as a sheep and weighs 100 pounds. So let's divide 4,738,500 pounds by 100. We see that there were about 47,385 animals on the ark.

Bible teachers have counted all the different species of animals in the world. They figured out that there only needed to be 16,000 animals on the ark! So there was *plenty* of room for *all* the animals that needed to be on board.

Do you understand the math for how many animals were on the ark?

Did you know we could figure out amazing facts like this?

46. WHY WAS ISRAEL CALLED THE PROMISED LAND?

\\\\\\\\\\\\\\\\\\\\\\\\

When Abraham first arrived in the land of Canaan, people called the Canaanites were already there. "Abram traveled through that land . . . . The Canaanites were living in the land at that time. The Lord appeared to Abram. The Lord said, 'I will give this land to your descendants'" (Genesis 12:6–7 ICB).

Later, God again promised to give Canaan to Abraham and his family (Genesis 13:14–15). God also promised it to his son Isaac. And He promised it to his grandson, Jacob (Genesis 26:3; 28:13–14). And He promised it to all the Israelites who came after them. Canaan was called "the Promised Land" because God promised it to the Israelites so often.

You may wonder, "But was it *right* to give Canaan to the Israelites when the Canaanites were already there?" The Israelites fought wars to drive the Canaanites out, and killed many of them. Yet the land *belonged* to the Canaanites, didn't it? No, it didn't. In fact, it didn't even belong to the Israelites.

God told the Israelites, "Your land. . .you do not own it; it belongs to God, and you are like foreigners who are allowed to make use of it" (Leviticus 25:23 GNT). *God* owned Canaan, and He let whoever He wanted live there. The

Canaanites had moved in without God's permission. So they had to leave.

In fact, the Canaanites were so wicked that God said He caused the land to vomit them out (Leviticus 18:25 NLT). Have you ever seen someone down on their hands and knees, heaving and vomiting? Canaan was heaving. Maybe this means it had lots of earthquakes. God had mercy on the Canaanites. He tried to make them flee. Then they wouldn't be there to fight and die.

That's why God did such great miracles. After God parted the Red Sea—and destroyed Egypt's chariot armies—Moses said, "The nations have heard, and they tremble with fear. . . . The people of Canaan lose their courage. Terror and dread fall upon them" (Exodus 15:14–16 GNT). And they *did* fear. Rahab told the spies, "We have heard how the LORD dried up the Red Sea. . . . We were afraid as soon as we heard about it" (Joshua 2:10–11 GNT).

God told the Israelites again and again to drive them out. He even sent hornets to drive the Canaanites out (Exodus 23:27–31; 34:11; Deuteronomy 7:1). The Canaanites could have simply moved south to Egypt. In fact, many of them did.

Why was Canaan called "the Promised Land"?

How could God just give the Canaanites' land to the Israelites?

47. WHY DID GOD TELL ABRAHAM TO KILL ISAAC?

\\\\\\\\\\\\\\\\\\\\\\\\\\\\\\

The Bible says, "Some time later, God tested Abraham's faith. 'Abraham!' God called. 'Yes,' he replied. 'Here I am.' 'Take your son, your only son—yes, Isaac, whom you love so much—and go to the land of Moriah. Go and sacrifice him as a burnt offering on one of the mountains, which I will show you.' The next morning Abraham got up early. He saddled his donkey and took two of his servants with him, along with his son, Isaac" (Genesis 22:1–3 NLT).

"When they arrived at the place where God had told him to go, Abraham built an altar and arranged the wood on it. Then he tied his son, Isaac, and laid him on the altar on top of the wood. And Abraham picked up the knife to kill his son as a sacrifice. At that moment the angel of the LORD called to him from heaven. . . . 'Do not hurt him in any way, for now I know that you truly fear God. You have not withheld from me even your son, your only son'" (vv. 9–12).

Most people get the lesson: Abraham loved God so much that he was willing to sacrifice the most precious thing he had—Isaac. But they're still horrified that he was willing to kill his son, then burn his body to ashes. But remember: Isaac wasn't in any danger no matter what Abraham did. If Abraham had refused to sacrifice him, Isaac would have lived. And even when Abraham was willing to sacrifice him, God made sure that Isaac lived.

And there's another lesson. "God made the promises to Abraham. But God tested him. And Abraham was ready to offer his own son as a sacrifice. God had said, 'The descendants I promised you will be from Isaac.' Abraham believed that God could raise the dead. And really, it was as if Abraham got Isaac back from death" (Hebrews 11:17–19 ICB). Abraham believed God could bring Isaac back to life after a knife wound—even after his dead body was burned to ashes.

God was testing Abraham. You might think He wanted to know if Abraham loved Him more than his son. But God already *knew* the answer to that question. God knows all things. He tested Abraham to show millions of believers down through the ages what was in his heart. God tested him for *your* sake! Abraham had great love for God *and* great faith in God.

How could Isaac have many descendants if Abraham killed Isaac?

Did God actually plan for Abraham to kill Isaac? Why do you think that?

48. WHY DID JACOB TRICK HIS FATHER ISAAC?

\\\\\\\\\\\\\\\\\\\\\\\\\\\\

Before Esau and Jacob were born, God made a promise to their mother Rebekah. God told her, "The sons in your womb will become two nations. From the very beginning, the two nations will be rivals. One nation will be stronger than the other; and your older son will serve your younger son" (Genesis 25:23 NLT). When Esau was born first, and Jacob born second, Rebekah knew that Esau would serve Jacob. Normally, the younger son served the older son. But this would be the other way round.

But as the two babies grew into men, Isaac ignored the prophecy. Because Esau was the older son, he had the birthright. That meant that he'd get most of the family's wealth, flocks, and land when Isaac died. But Esau didn't value the birthright. One day he came home from hunting and was very hungry. He traded his birthright to Jacob for one bowl of lentils.

Of course, Rebekah told Isaac that Esau had sold his birthright to Jacob. So Isaac *should* have then given the blessing to Jacob. But Isaac had made up his mind to give it to Esau. He liked to eat the wild antelope Esau hunted. Esau was his favorite son. So one day, when he thought Rebekah wasn't listening, Isaac sent Esau out hunting. He told him to hunt and cook some antelope, and bring it to him. Then Isaac would bless him.

But Rebekah was listening. And she panicked! She thought she had to do something. So she cooked two young goats. Then she dressed Jacob in Esau's robes. Isaac was blind, so he couldn't see that it was Jacob coming into his tent with the food. Jacob copied Esau's voice and lied that he was Esau. Isaac believed Jacob, and gave him the blessing.

Jacob was *supposed* to get the blessing and birthright—but not by lying! Not by tricking his dad! God had promised that Jacob would rule his family. But Rebekah and Jacob didn't trust God could keep His promise. So they thought *they* had to do something—and quickly! So they tricked Isaac into giving the blessing to Jacob.

God could have done it another way if they had trusted Him. If you ever get in a jam where you think you have to steal or lie. . .think again. "Be patient and wait for the LORD to act. . . . Don't give in to worry or anger; it only leads to trouble" (Psalm 37:7–8 GNT).

Was God able to give Jacob the blessing an honest way?

Have you ever felt tempted to lie to your parents or deceive them?

49. WHY DID JOSEPH'S BROTHERS SELL HIM AS A SLAVE?

\\\\\\\\\\\\\\\\\\

Jacob had four wives, but Rachel was the prettiest, and Jacob loved her more than the others. Jacob had twelve sons, but only his two youngest sons—Joseph and Benjamin—were from Rachel. Then Rachel died and Jacob missed her. So he loved her two sons more than his other ten sons.

He also loved them more because they were born when he was old. He couldn't do hard work anymore, so he often stayed in the camp with these two sons. He hadn't spent *that* much time with his ten older sons.

When Joseph was seventeen, he helped his brothers watch the flocks. "But Joseph reported to his father some of the bad things his brothers were doing. . . . So one day Jacob had a special gift made for Joseph—a beautiful robe." As a result, "his brothers hated Joseph. . . . They couldn't say a kind word to him" (Genesis 37:2–4 NLT).

Then Joseph had dreams that showed that his brothers would bow down to him. His dreams later came true, but Joseph made a big mistake. He should have kept them to himself. But he couldn't resist telling his brothers. They asked, "So you think you will be our king, do you?" (v. 8). And they hated him even more.

One day, Joseph's brothers saw him coming their way and decided to kill him. They ripped his robe off him and threw him in a pit. But then they saw some merchants riding by on camels. So they sold Joseph to them. The merchants took him to Egypt and sold him as a slave. Meanwhile, Joseph's brothers dipped his robe in goat's blood and sent it to their father. Jacob thought Joseph had been killed by a wild animal.

But after Joseph was a slave in Egypt for several years, God did something amazing. Pharaoh had two mysterious dreams. After Joseph told him what his dreams meant, Pharaoh gave Joseph a very important job. He stored up tons and tons of grain to save the world from a great famine. Next to Pharaoh, Joseph was the most powerful ruler in Egypt.

This sad story finally had a happy ending. Joseph saved Egypt from the famine. Joseph even brought his whole family from Canaan to save them too. And Joseph told his brothers, "You intended to harm me, but God intended it all for good. He brought me to this position so I could save the lives of many people" (Genesis 50:20 NLT).

What mistake did Joseph make?

Has God ever brought good out of a bad situation for *you*? How?

50. WHY DID GOD LET JOB SUFFER SO MUCH?

\\\\\\\\\\\\\\\\\\\\\

Have you heard of the story of Job? He was a righteous man who lived in the land of Uz. Job was very rich. Then in *one day* Job lost all his wealth. Robbers stole all his oxen and donkeys and camels. A lightning storm killed all his sheep. A terrific windstorm killed his sons and daughters. Job was filled with grief. He knew that these things hadn't happened by chance. God Himself had allowed them. Then things got worse! Job's body was covered with painful, ugly sores. He suffered for months. And Job had nightmares every night (see Job 1:13–22; 7:3–5,13–15).

Why did God let Job suffer so much? Job couldn't understand. He had obeyed God's commands. He had sacrificed animals and prayed for the Lord to protect his family. So why had God let these terrible things happen?

Back then, people believed that sin always caused suffering. *Always.* If people saw you suffering, they would say, "Aha! You must have sinned!" If you were sick, God was punishing some sin. If you had an accident, God was punishing some sin. So Job's friends said, "Stop sinning and God will bless you again" (see Job 11:13–19). But Job said he hadn't sinned. That made his friends mad. A man named Eliphaz then accused Job of doing terrible things (see Job 22:5–11).

Yes, sometimes people *do* sin and God *does* judge them for it. But that wasn't the reason this time. So why did the Lord allow Job to suffer? God allowed it to prove to the devil that Job loved God—no matter *what* happened to him. And the things Job suffered purified him. Job said, "*When* He has tested me, I shall come forth as gold" (Job 23:10 NKJV). Job went through fiery tests to burn impure things out of his heart.

And God blessed Job afterwards (see Job 42:10–17). The Bible says, "For examples of patience in suffering, dear brothers and sisters, look at the prophets. . . . For instance, you know about Job. . . . You can see how the Lord was kind to him at the end, for the Lord is full of tenderness and mercy" (James 5:10–11 NLT).

It's not easy for God to watch you suffer. Just like any good parent, it hurts Him to see you in pain. "He may bring us sorrow, but his love for us is sure and strong. He takes no pleasure in causing us grief or pain" (Lamentations 3:32–33 GNT).

Why were Job's friends so sure that he must have sinned?

What good did God get out of letting Job suffer?

51. DID THE RED SEA REALLY SPLIT APART SO THE ISRAELITES COULD CROSS?

\\\\\\\\\\\\\\\\\\\\\\\

Yes! It did. The Israelites had been slaves in Egypt, and Pharaoh finally told Moses they could leave. So all the men, women, and children went together. Then Pharaoh said, "What have we done? We have let the Israelites escape, and we have lost them as our slaves!" (Exodus 14:5 GNT). Pharaoh jumped in his chariot and led six hundred other war chariots after the Israelites. They caught up to them just before sunset. The Israelites were by the Red Sea. They were trapped!

Then, "Moses held out his hand over the sea, and the LORD drove the sea back with a strong east wind. It blew all night and turned the sea into dry land. The water was divided, and the Israelites went through the sea on dry ground, with walls of water on both sides. The Egyptians pursued them and went after them into the sea with all their horses, chariots, and drivers" (vv. 21–23).

Just before dawn, God made the Egyptians' chariot wheels get stuck, so they couldn't escape. Then, after the last Israelite stepped out of the sea, God made the walls of water come crashing down. All the Egyptians were drowned.

This was a *great* miracle! Hundreds of years later, the Israelites were still talking about it. Just read the Psalms. But you notice that God used natural things to create this miracle. The Bible says, "the LORD drove the sea back with a strong east wind." And the same wind "blew all night" (v. 21).

The Reed Sea is north of the Red Sea, and even today, strong winds often blow its shallow water apart. Then Arabs cross it on dry land. But God did a much bigger, greater miracle for the Israelites.

In the next chapter, Miriam, Moses' sister, said, "By the blast of your nostrils the waters piled up. The surging waters stood up like a wall; the deep waters congealed in the heart of the sea" (Exodus 15:8 NIV). What does "congealed" mean? Well, another Bible translation says: "the deepest part of the sea became solid" (GNT). And another translation says, "in the heart of the sea the deep waters became hard" (NLT).

Water normally becomes hard and solid when it gets very cold. It turns into ice. So did God freeze the walls of water solid? We don't know. He could have done that if He'd chosen to. For sure, He was doing *something* amazing.

- -

How did God use the wind to part the Red Sea?

Could God have made the water "hard" and
  "solid" without freezing it?

52. WHY DID THE ISRAELITES COMPLAIN SO MUCH?

\\\\\\\\\\\\\\\\\\\\\\\\\\

The main reason the Israelites complained was because they didn't believe God loved them. They didn't trust He would take care of them. If you don't believe God loves you, then you're in trouble. It's easy to think that He hates you, and is trying to wreck your life. That's what the Israelites thought.

Not long after leaving Egypt, they ran out of food. They moaned that they should have stayed in Egypt. They complained to God and Moses, "There we sat around pots filled with meat and ate all the bread we wanted. But now you have brought us into this wilderness to starve us all to death" (Exodus 16:3 NLT). But what did God do to show His love? He supplied delicious manna—*for the next forty years*!

Sometime after, "They camped at Rephidim, but there was no water to drink. . . . The people were very thirsty and continued to complain to Moses. They said, 'Why did you bring us out of Egypt? To kill us and our children and our livestock with thirst?'" (Exodus 17:1-3 GNT). Again they thought the very worst. They thought God was out to kill them. But God *loved* them and did a miracle. Moses hit a rock with his staff, and water poured out of the rock.

Later, the Israelites whined, "In Egypt we used to eat all the fish we wanted. . . . Remember the cucumbers, the watermelons, the leeks, the onions, and the garlic we had? But now our strength is gone. There is nothing at all to eat—nothing but this manna day after day!" (Numbers 11:5–6 GNT). But what did God do? He proved He *loved* them by sending tons and tons of quail to eat.

Another reason the Israelites complained was because they didn't believe God was *able* to provide. This was after He had done a miracle to give them water. They asked, "Can God prepare food in the desert? When he hit the rock, water poured out. Rivers flowed down. But can he give us bread also? Will he provide his people with meat?" (Psalm 78:19–20 ICB). Of course He could. And He did.

Don't criticize the Israelites for complaining. Instead, learn from their sad example. You're probably tempted to complain often too. Make up your mind not to whine. Trust God to take care of you. Remind yourself of all the good things He does for you. Be thankful. And praise Him.

What should you do when you feel like complaining?

If you need God to do a miracle for you, do you trust He can do one?

53. WHAT MADE THE ARK OF THE COVENANT SO SPECIAL?

\\\\\\\\\\\\\\\\\\\\\\\

The ark of the covenant was a wooden box. It was less than four feet long, and it was a little over two feet high and two feet wide. But it was the most valuable wooden box on earth.

People also call wooden boxes like that chests. When pirates put treasure in them, they call them treasure chests. The ark of the covenant was the most valuable treasure chest in the universe. Pirate's chests are filled with thousands of gold and silver coins. What was in *this* chest? Two stone tablets with God's law, the Ten Commandments, written on them. A Psalmist wrote, "The law from your mouth is more precious to me than thousands of pieces of silver and gold" (Psalm 119:72 NIV).

God told Moses to make this chest out of wood. Then He said: "Cover it with pure gold inside and out.... Make a lid of pure gold.... Make two winged creatures [cherubim] of hammered gold, one for each end of the lid. Make them so that they form one piece with the lid. The winged creatures are to face each other across the lid.... I will meet you there, and from above the lid between the two winged creatures I will give you all my laws for the people of Israel" (Exodus 25:11, 17–20, 22 GNT).

What made the ark of the covenant so holy? It wasn't because it was covered with gold. God has tons of gold. Where He lives, the *streets* are made of gold (Revelation 21:21). It was holy because God promised, "I will meet you there." In the desert, God often came down to the ark with His glory. Then He spoke to the Israelites from between the two cherubim (see Numbers 7:89). He made it holy.

One day the Philistines captured the ark. Then they boasted that their god was more powerful than God. They put the ark of the covenant in Dagon's temple. Big mistake. Dagon's idol fell down in front of the ark. Then, in every city the Philistines took the ark to, many Philistines died (see 1 Samuel 4:1–11; 5:1–12).

The Philistines became terrified of the ark of the covenant. So they sent it back to Israel. But some Israelites at Beth Shemesh failed to respect God. They lifted the lid of the ark and seventy men peeked inside. For that sin, they died (see 1 Samuel 6:19).

What made the ark of the covenant so special?

Why weren't people allowed to look inside it?

54. WHY WAS GOD SO ANGRY IN MOSES' TIME?

\\\\\\\\\\\\\\\\\\\\\\\\\\

In the New Testament, the apostle John wrote, "God is love" (1 John 4:18). And Paul talks about how "the kindness and love of God our Savior was shown" (Titus 3:4 ICB). But the Old Testament often describes God as angry. It seems that God was mad *much* of the time. Every time the Israelites complained, God became angry and punished them.

The angriest He ever got was at Mount Sinai after the Israelites made a golden calf and worshipped it. Moses told the Israelites later, "At Mount Sinai you made the LORD angry—angry enough to destroy you" (Deuteronomy 9:8 GNT). God was so furious He told Moses, "Don't try to stop me. I intend to destroy them so that no one will remember them any longer" (v. 14). Moses later told the Israelites, "I was afraid of the LORD's fierce anger, because he was furious enough to destroy you. . . . The LORD was also angry enough with Aaron to kill him" (v. 19–20).

Some people think God was a god of vengeance, punishment, and anger in the Old Testament. Then He became a God of love, compassion, and mercy in the New Testament. Many people ask, "Why did God change?"

He didn't change. God said, "I am the Lord. I do not change" (Malachi 3:6 ICB). Jonah described

God in Old Testament days, saying, "I knew that you are a God who is kind and shows mercy. You don't become angry quickly. You have great love. I knew you would rather forgive than punish them" (Jonah 4:2 ICB). God was already loving and kind in the Old Testament.

And God and His Son Jesus Christ still get angry in New Testament times. They still take vengeance against the wicked. Paul said Jesus will come back "from heaven with his powerful angels. He will come from heaven with burning fire to punish those who do not know God. He will punish those who do not obey the Good News of our Lord Jesus Christ. Those people will be punished with a destruction that continues forever. They will not be allowed to be with the Lord" (2 Thessalonians 1:7–9 ICB).

So why did God get angry in Moses' day? The stubborn, rebellious people *made* Him angry. Moses explained, "Never forget how you made the Lord your God angry in the desert. From the day that you left Egypt until the day you arrived here, you have rebelled against him" (Deuteronomy 9:7 GNT).

- -

Was God already a loving, kind God in Old Testament times?

Does God sometimes still get angry in New Testament times?

55. HOW COULD BALAAM'S DONKEY TALK?

\\\\\\\\\\\\\\\\\\\\\\\\\\\\

There once was a prophet named Balaam. He received some true prophecies, but Balaam was also greedy for money. Once, the king of Moab offered Balaam a room full of gold if he would curse the Israelites. God didn't want Balaam to go with the king's men. But Balaam went anyway.

So God sent an angel with a sword to kill Balaam. The donkey saw the angel and ran off the road into a field. Balaam couldn't see the angel, so he hit his donkey and made it go back to the road. Then the angel stood in the road between two vineyards. So the donkey moved to one side and scraped Balaam's foot against a wall. The king's men laughed. They thought Balaam had a poorly-trained donkey. So Balaam hit his donkey again.

Then the angel stood in a narrow place. There was no room to squeeze past it on either side. So the donkey lay down in the road. Then the king's men really laughed. Balaam got angry and beat the donkey with a stick.

Then God opened the donkey's mouth. It said to Balaam, "What have I done to make you hit me three times?"

Balaam answered, "You have made me look foolish! I wish I had a sword in my hand! I would kill you right now!"

The donkey said, "I am your very own donkey. You have ridden me for years. Have I ever done this to you before?"

"No," Balaam said (Numbers 22:28–30 ICB). Then God opened Balaam's eyes, and he saw the fierce angel with a sword. So Balaam bowed down.

You shouldn't be too surprised by a donkey talking. Lots of birds are good at speaking human languages. For example: Budgies, Hill Mynas, Amazon Parrots, African Grey Parrots, Cockatoos, Crows, European Starlings, Mockingbirds, Lyrebirds, Magpies, and Jays. N'kisi (an African Grey Parrot) can speak over 950 words. Yet birds' brains are so small! Plus, their mouths aren't made for speaking. Their beaks can't form words like human lips. Even donkeys can move their mouths more. So how do birds *do* it? With their throats and tongues.

Some people think it's impossible for a donkey to talk. Their brains aren't smart enough. Well, their brains are much bigger than birds' brains. But even if they could think of things to say, donkey's mouths aren't used to speaking. It would take a miracle for them to speak. Well, that's what it *was*—a miracle.

- -

Is God able to do a miracle and make a donkey speak human words?

Why did God have to do such a miracle?

56. HOW DID GOD DRY UP THE JORDAN RIVER?

\\\\\\\\\\\\\\\\\\\\\\\\\\\\\

Joshua and the Israelite army stood on the banks of the Jordan River. They needed to cross over to Jericho. Normally, the Jordan isn't very wide, but it was springtime. Mountain snow was melting, and heavy rain was falling. This made the river overflow its banks and flood the whole valley. Joshua had shown up at the worst possible time. Nobody was crossing the river. The people of Jericho laughed at them.

But the second the Israelite priests stepped into the river carrying the ark of the covenant, the water started to drain away. Soon all the water was gone. Then the Israelite army began crossing. The priests stood in the riverbed while the army crossed over. Then, seconds after the priests stepped up out of the riverbed, the river began to roar, full of water again. When the Canaanites saw this, their "hearts melted in fear and they no longer had the courage to face the Israelites" (Joshua 5:1 NIV).

How did God do this miracle? Joshua 3:16 (NLT) tells us that "the water above that point began backing up a great distance away at a town called Adam. . . . And the water below that point flowed on to the Dead Sea until the riverbed was dry."

The town of Adam is thirty miles north of

Jericho. The river gorge is narrow there. In 1927, the cliffs collapsed and fell into the Jordan River. This blocked up the river. No water flowed past the dam of rocks for twenty hours.

God probably caused a landslide like that in Joshua's day. And what caused the cliffs to collapse into the river? Psalm 114:3–7 (GNT) says, "The Jordan River stopped flowing. The mountains skipped like goats; the hills jumped around like lambs. . . . And you, O Jordan, why did you stop flowing? You mountains, why did you skip like goats? You hills, why did you jump around like lambs? Tremble, earth, at the Lord's coming."

It's clear from these verses that God sent an earthquake that made the hills and mountains shake. Then the cliff fell into the river. Even though He used natural means to dry up the river, talk about exact timing! That was a huge miracle!

While the Israelites were still crossing, the Jordan River burst over the rocks upriver at Adam. Then a flood roared downriver toward the Israelites. And the second the last priest walked out of the riverbed, the river was full again. No wonder the Canaanites were scared.

- -

Can God use an earthquake and a landslide to make a miracle?

When have things happened at a *perfect time* in your life?

57. DID THE WALLS OF JERICHO REALLY FALL DOWN? HOW DID THEY?

\\\\\\\\\\\\\\\\\\\\\\\\\

Yes. The walls of Jericho really did fall down. After the Israelite army had marched around Jericho seven times, "the people shouted when the priests blew the trumpets. And. . .the wall fell down flat" (Joshua 6:20 NKJV).

Scientists called archaeologists [*arc-ee-ol-*oh-gists] dig up ruins of old cities to learn about the past. From 1930–1936, an archaeologist named John Garstrang dug at the place where the ancient city of Jericho had been. Here's what he found:

The Bible says that "the wall fell down flat" (6:20). Garstrang found that all of Jericho's walls *had* fallen. And they fell outwards, *away* from the city.

The Bible says that Rahab's "house was on the city wall; she dwelt on the wall" (2:15). In most ancient cities, houses were built *away* from the walls. But Jericho's houses were built right against the outer walls.

The Bible says that the Israelites "burned the city and all that was in it with fire" (6:24). Garstrang found piles of burned wood, ashes, and burned bricks, over three feet deep.

The Bible says that Joshua attacked Jericho in spring (3:15). Ancient Jericho *was* destroyed in early spring after harvest. We know this because

Garstrang found huge jars full of wheat, barley, dates, and lentils.

The Bible says that the Israelites surrounded Jericho, and the people couldn't get out for seven days. "But the seventh day. . .the wall of the city will fall down flat" (6:4–5). Since so many jars of food were full, we know that the people of Jericho weren't trapped in their city very long.

So how did the walls fall down flat? Some people say that if you play a violin just right, you can make a steel bridge vibrate so much that it falls down. (That may or may *not* be true.) So they say that maybe when the Israelites shouted and blew trumpets, the noise vibrated Jericho's walls just right, and made them fall. But was it that easy to bring down stone walls? No. If it was, the Israelites would have done that to *all* the cities of Canaan they fought against. But they didn't.

Probably God used another earthquake to make the walls of Jericho come tumbling down. The Lord had just stopped the Jordan River with an earthquake a few days earlier. Again, what a miracle of timing! God sent an earthquake at the exact same time as the trumpets blew and the Israelites shouted!

How does archaeology prove that the Bible is true?

What is the most amazing thing about Jericho's walls falling?

58. WHY DID BIBLE PEOPLE FIGHT AND KILL THEIR ENEMIES?

\\\\\\\\\\\\\\\\\\\\\\\\

When you read stories about Joshua and the later kings of Israel, you notice one thing right away. They fought many wars against their enemies. Their soldiers often marched out, armed with swords. And they used those weapons to kill enemy soldiers.

But in the New Testament, Jesus said, "Love your enemies. Do good to those who hate you" (Luke 6:27 ICB). Does that mean that Christian soldiers shouldn't fight? Should they throw down their guns and give flowers to enemy soldiers instead?

And what about when Peter pulled out a sword to protect Jesus? He told Peter, "Put away your sword. Those who use the sword will die by the sword" (Matthew 26:52 NLT). Was Jesus telling all soldiers and policemen to put away *their* weapons? No. Jesus was telling Peter that He needed to die on the cross. So Peter shouldn't try to stop the mob of men from arresting Him. If Peter had got in their way, they would have just killed him.

What about when the Roman soldiers repented and asked John the Baptist what they should do? John answered, "Do violence to no man" (Luke 3:14 KJV). Fighting and waging war is violence. So was John telling soldiers they weren't supposed to fight wars anymore?

No. The Greek word that the KJV Bible translates as "violence" actually means "to shake someone." In John's day, many Roman soldiers were greedy. They weren't content with their wages. So they grabbed people, shook them, and said, "Give me some money or I'll hurt you." John told them to stop doing that. That's why modern Bibles translate this verse: "Don't take money from anyone by force or accuse anyone falsely. Be content with your pay" (Luke 3:14 GNT).

The fact is, Christian policemen still use weapons to protect you from criminals. Godly soldiers still use guns to protect your country from its enemies. That hasn't changed from the Old Testament to the New Testament.

Paul wrote: "Those who do right do not have to fear the rulers. But people who do wrong must fear them. Do you want to be unafraid of the rulers? Then do what is right. . . . But if you do wrong, then be afraid. The ruler has the power to punish; he is God's servant to punish those who do wrong" (Romans 13:3–4 ICB). Soldiers and policemen work for their rulers. They're serving God when they "carry a sword" to protect your country. So respect them.

Why did John tell the soldiers, "Do violence to no man"?

Why is it right for policemen and soldiers to have weapons and use them?

59. DID THE SUN ACTUALLY STAND STILL WHEN JOSHUA PRAYED?

\\\\\\\\\\\\\\\\\\\\\\\\

Yes, it did. This happened when the Israelites were taking over Canaan. There was a city named Gibeon. Its people had agreed to make peace with Israel. This made the Amorite kings of Canaan angry. So they sent their armies to attack Gibeon. But Joshua marched to Gibeon, and began fighting the Amorites.

The Israelites fought all day. Finally, the sun was almost setting, and the moon appeared. Joshua's army was winning, so he wanted to finish the battle. But they couldn't fight in the dark. So Joshua prayed, "Sun, stand still over Gibeon. And you, moon, stand still over the Valley of Aijalon." So the sun stood still, and the moon stopped. The Bible says, "The sun. . .waited to go down for a full day. That has never happened at any time before that day or since. That was the day the Lord listened to a man" (Joshua 10:12–14 icb).

The sun didn't move for about twelve hours. How did God do this? Well, He didn't answer Joshua's prayer the way he expected. But He knew what Joshua *meant*.

Joshua thought the sun circled around the earth. That's what people in his day believed. But God makes the earth to go around the sun. But the earth also rotates—it spins like a giant ball.

This makes it seem like the sun travels across the sky and sets. So did the earth suddenly stop rotating? No. That would've caused great earthquakes and tidal waves. It would have killed all life on the planet.

So what happened? We don't know, because God didn't tell us. But think about this: we know that God created earth and the universe. He created four dimensions: length, width, depth, and time. Scientists call this the *space-time continuum*. Normally, it's woven together, like threads of four different colors in one blanket.

But on this day at Gibeon, God froze time for about twelve hours. It was like the rest of the world was standing still. Have you ever seen a movie were someone stops time? The heroes walk among people who are frozen in the middle of doing something. Time stopped. But meanwhile, the Israelites and the Amorites kept fighting for about twelve hours. Then, when the Israelites had won, God started time moving again.

Does that sound like a *huge* miracle? You bet it was! But God is the One who created the space-time continuum. So He's able to make it work differently sometimes if He wants to.

Why has there never been another day like
  this day?

How do you think God froze the sun and moon
  in the sky?

60. HOW DID SAMSON'S LONG HAIR MAKE HIM SO STRONG?

\\\\\\\\\\\\\\\\\\\\\\

It wasn't Samson's long hair that made him so strong. It was the Spirit of God. Often, Israelite men and women wanted to spend more time praying. So they would become Nazirites. Nazirites didn't drink wine or eat grapes—even grape skins. And they didn't cut their hair. Then, after they had drawn close to God, people went back to their normal lives. They stopped being Nazirites. Then they ate grapes and cut their hair again.

The angel told Samson's mother, "You must never cut his hair because he will be a Nazirite. He will be given to God from birth" (Judges 13:5 ICB). Samson wasn't just a Nazirite for a few weeks or months. He was a Nazirite his *entire life*. That's why his hair could *never* be cut. God's law said:

"During the time he promised to belong to the Lord, he must not cut his hair. He must be holy until this special time is over. He must let his hair grow long.... He must still keep his promise to belong to God in a special way. While he is a Nazirite, he belongs to the Lord " (Numbers 6:5, 7–8 ICB).

The hair on Samson's head showed people that he was set apart for God. And his long hair reminded him that he was holy. Whenever Samson thought about his hair, it made him think of God. It reminded him to pray—to praise God and to depend on Him. That's why the Spirit of God often came over Samson and gave him great strength.

The Bible says, "Suddenly, a young lion came roaring toward Samson! The Spirit of the Lord entered Samson with great power. Samson tore the lion apart with his bare hands." Later, "the Spirit of the Lord entered Samson and gave him great power. . . . Samson found a jawbone of a donkey that had just died. He took it and killed 1,000 men with it!" (Judges 14:5–6; 15:14–15 ICB).

Samson lost his great strength when Delilah cut his hair, breaking the promise. Samson was no longer a Nazirite, holy and set apart for God. But when his hair grew back, he was a Nazirite again. Then God gave him great strength once more (see Judges 16:17–20, 22–30).

- -

What gave Samson great strength? His hair? Not eating grapes? God's Spirit?

How can God use *you* if you set yourself apart for Him?

61. WERE THERE REALLY GIANTS IN BIBLE TIMES?

\\\\\\\\\\\\\\\\\\\\\\\\\\

Yes, there certainly were giants long ago! And they were monster-sized! Giants like Goliath were 9 feet 9 inches tall (1 Samuel 17:4) and probably weighed about 850 pounds of solid muscle. Giants like Og were even bigger! They were about 11 feet tall (Deuteronomy 3:11) and weighed around 1,200 pounds.

Back in Joshua's day, there were hundreds of giants—maybe even thousands of them. The Bible says several times that giants were "numerous" in Canaan. And they were divided into six great clans. There were the Anakim of the hills of southern Canaan (Joshua 14:15); the Avvim of the sea coast (Deuteronomy 2:23); the Emim of Moab (Deuteronomy 2:10–11); the Zamzummim of Ammon (Deuteronomy 2:20–21); the Rephaim of Bashan (Deuteronomy 3:11, 13); and the Rephaim of northern Canaan (Joshua 17:15).

Giants were scary and scary-looking. But God made a promise to the Israelites: "The people themselves are tall and strong; they are giants, and you have heard it said that no one can stand against them. But now you will see for yourselves that the LORD your God will. . .defeat them as you advance, so that you will drive them out and destroy them quickly, as he promised" (Deuteronomy 9:2–3 GNT).

Sure enough, "Joshua went and destroyed the race of giants called the Anakim who lived in the hill country—in Hebron, Debir, Anab. . . . Joshua completely destroyed them and their cities. None of the Anakim were left in the land of Israel; a few, however, were left in Gaza, Gath, and Ashdod" (Joshua 11:21–22 GNT).

Giant-killers like Joshua, Caleb, and Othniel slew most of the giants. The ones who survived fled to the land of the Philistines. That's why Goliath showed up in Gath four hundred years later. By David's day, Goliath and his sons were the only giants left.

Goliath is the most famous giant, because we know the most about him. He wore bronze armor that weighed 125 pounds, and the iron head of his spear weighed 15 pounds (1 Samuel 17:5, 7). He was a trained warrior and very powerful! But there were other Bible giants like Anak, Ahiman, Sheshai, Talmai, Ishi-Benob, Saph, and Lahmi. We know a bit about their terrifying adventures too. The giant Ishbi-Benob, for example, tried to kill King David.

(If you want to read more about giants, order the book, *Big Bad Bible Giants* by Ed Strauss.)

Did you know there were giants in the Bible?

Are there "giants" in your life that you need
  God's help to conquer?

62. CAN I PRAY FOR GREAT WISDOM LIKE SOLOMON DID?

\\\\\\\\\\\\\\\\\\\\\\\\\

Some people think Christians must have easier lives than other people. After all, God's Holy Spirit lives in their hearts. So isn't life always wonderful? Aren't they happy all the time? You know that that's not so. Things still go wrong. You often have problems. Sometimes, you get frustrated. You don't know what to do. At times, you really need wisdom to know what's happening.

Or your schoolwork may be very difficult this year. And you may wish you didn't have to work so hard to get the right answers to all those questions. You wish you could simply pray and God would give you a huge download of knowledge. Yippee! Then you wouldn't need to study. You could spend all your time playing. *You wish...*

But didn't Solomon pray for wisdom? Yes, he did. God appeared to Solomon in a dream during the night. God said, "Ask for anything you want. I will give it to you." Solomon answered in the dream, "Lord my God, you have allowed me to be king in my father's place. But I am like a little child. I do not have the wisdom I need to do what I must do. So I ask that you give me wisdom. Then I can rule the people in the right way. Then I will know the difference between right and wrong."

God was very pleased that Solomon had asked for wisdom. So He told Solomon, "Since you asked for wisdom to make the right decisions, I will give you what you asked. I will give you wisdom and understanding" (1 Kings 3:5, 7, 9–12 ICB).

If you're praying for God to give you more wisdom and to make you wiser than you are, God will definitely answer your prayers. So pray and *keep* praying! The Bible promises, "If you need wisdom, ask our generous God, and he will give it to you. He will not rebuke you for asking" (James 1:5 NLT). God will give it to you generously. And He won't scold you for asking. He *wants* you to ask!

But remember, you'll still need to study and learn. When Daniel and his friends went to school in Babylon, "God gave these four men wisdom and the ability to learn. They learned many kinds of things people had written and studied" (Daniel 1:17 ICB). But they still had to do *their* part and study.

Has God promised to give you wisdom if you ask? How *much* wisdom?

How do you work *with* God to gain wisdom and knowledge?

63. HOW DID WASHING IN A RIVER HEAL NAAMAN OF LEPROSY?

\\\\\\\\\\\\\\\\\\\\\\\\\\\\\\

Long ago, Ben-Hadad was king of Aram. The commander of his army was a mighty warrior named Naaman. God used Naaman to give Aram great victories. Aram had fought many wars with Israel also.

Naaman suffered from leprosy. Then he heard there was a prophet in Israel who could heal him. So he went to Elisha's house. Elisha sent out a messenger who said, "Go and wash yourself seven times in the Jordan River. Then. . .you will be healed of your leprosy."

But Naaman became angry. "Aren't the rivers of Damascus, the Abana and the Pharpar, better than any of the rivers of Israel? Why shouldn't I wash in them and be healed?" So Naaman stomped off in a rage.

But Naaman's officers said, "Sir, if the prophet had told you to do something very difficult, wouldn't you have done it? So you should certainly obey him when he says simply, 'Go and wash and be cured!'" So Naaman went down to the Jordan River and washed seven times. And he was *healed*! (2 Kings 5:10–14 NLT).

The water in the Jordan River wasn't miraculous. It never healed anyone else, before or after. In fact, they were sometimes a bit muddy. That's why

Naaman didn't want to wash in the Jordan River. The rivers of Aram were cleaner. But God wanted to humble this proud commander.

When Naaman obeyed God, he was healed. That was very similar to the ten lepers Jesus healed. One day, Jesus met ten men with leprosy. They shouted, "Jesus, Master, have pity on us!" Jesus said, "Go, show yourselves to the priests." And as they obeyed Jesus and went, they were healed (Luke 17:13–14 NIV).

You may wonder why God healed an enemy like Naaman. The Jews wondered the same thing. They thought they were the only people God loved. But Jesus said, "Many in Israel had leprosy in the time of the prophet Elisha, but the only one healed was Naaman, a Syrian" (Luke 4:27 NLT). Jesus was saying that God loved everyone.

Think about this too: Ben-Hadad, king of Aram, was an enemy of Israel. He often sent his army to fight against them. God wanted him to be at peace with Israel. God knew that healing Naaman would show His power to Ben-Hadad. But Elisha's servant, Gehazi, disobeyed God. And later Naaman disobeyed God by bowing to another god. So the peace between Aram and Israel didn't last as long as it would have.

Why did Naaman have to wash in the Jordan River to be healed?

Why did God heal one of Israel's worst enemies?

64. HOW COULD A FISH BE BIG ENOUGH TO SWALLOW JONAH?

\\\\\\\\\\\\\\\\\\\\\\\\\\\\

The Assyrians were the most violent, cruel empire the world had ever seen, and Jonah knew this. So at first he was happy when God told him to go to Nineveh and preach, "Forty days from now Nineveh will be destroyed!" (Jonah 3:4 NLT). Then Jonah realized that the Assyrians might repent if they heard this warning. Then God would have mercy and not destroy them. So Jonah took a ship in the opposite direction. He wanted to make sure Nineveh would be destroyed.

You know what happened next: God sent a storm and the sailors threw Jonah into the sea. He was swallowed by a great sea monster, which finally vomited him up on the shore. And once again God ordered Jonah to warn Nineveh. This time he obeyed.

The Bible says, "And the Lord caused a very big fish to swallow Jonah. Jonah was in the stomach of the fish three days and three nights" (Jonah 1:17 ICB). Many people wonder if there are actually fish big enough to swallow a man. The only fish they know are the tiny tropical fish in their aquarium. But there are some truly *monstrous fish* out there! And there were even *more* in the past.

Some marine scientists from Sea World in San Diego said that probably a great white shark swallowed Jonah. These sharks can grow 20 feet long and weigh up to 4,300 pounds. Whale sharks are even larger. They can grow up to 41.5 feet long and weigh 47,000 pounds.

This "fish" could also have been a whale. When Jesus talked about Jonah, He said that Jonah was in the belly of "a great sea monster" (Matthew 12:40). That's what the Greek word *ketos* means. The Blue Whale and the Sperm Whale are both monstrous. Both have big enough throats to swallow a man.

But people ask, "What about the digestive juices? Wouldn't Jonah have been killed by a shark's or a whale's stomach acids?" No. When whales swallow food, it goes through two stomachs. The first stomach crushes the food. In the second chamber, digestive juices break the food down. If Jonah stayed in the first stomach, he wouldn't have had stomach acid on him. Maybe that's why the great sea monster finally vomited him up. He wasn't digesting.

And good news if a shark swallowed him! Sharks take their time digesting. Jonah could have gone three days without getting covered with stomach acid.

What do you think the "great sea monster" was that swallowed Jonah?

Why do you think Jonah wasn't digested in its stomach?

65. WHY DIDN'T THE JEWS LIKE THE SAMARITANS?

\\\\\\\\\\\\\\\\\\\\\\\\\\\\\\\

In Jesus' day, the land of Samaria was between Judea and Galilee. In the centuries before that, Israelites from the tribes of Ephraim and Manasseh lived there. But the Assyrians took most of the Israelites from their land. They settled them in faraway lands. Then the Assyrians put new people from Babylon in their place. These new people married the few Israelites still living there. The main city of the land was Samaria. So these people became known as Samaritans.

At first, these new people worshipped their own gods. They didn't worship the Lord. So God sent lions among them, and the lions killed several of them. Then the king of Assyria brought some Israelite priests back to that land. The priests taught the new people to worship the Lord. Then the lions left them alone. But the Samaritans worshipped the Lord *plus* their old gods (see 2 Kings 17:24–29).

In Zerubbabel's day, the Jews returned to Judah and rebuilt their temple. The Samaritans wanted to help them, but the Jews wouldn't let them (see Ezra 4:1–3). They didn't want the Samaritans to worship at their temple with them. So the Samaritans built their own temple on Mount Gerizim, near Samaria. They worshipped God there (John 4:20).

Later, the Greeks ruled Judea and Samaria.

The Samaritans were afraid of the Greeks. So they began to worship the Greek god Zeus in their temple. This made the Jews so mad they later tore down the Samaritan's temple.

In Jesus' day, the Jews wouldn't even use the same dishes Samaritans used. That's why the Samaritan woman was surprised that Jesus asked her for a drink of water. "Jews refuse to have anything to do with Samaritans" (John 4:9 NLT). They believed that the Samaritans were "unclean." When the religious leaders wanted to insult Jesus, the worst thing they could think to say about Him was, "You Samaritan devil! Didn't we say all along that you were possessed by a demon?" (John 8:48 NLT).

Jesus told the story of the good Samaritan to show that Samaritans could be true followers of God (Luke 10:30–35). Later, Jesus' disciples preached the Gospel in Samaria. And many Samaritans became Christians.

Many people today dislike people who are different from them. They're prejudiced against people of another race, or who worship God differently from them. But Jesus wants you to love foreigners like you love your neighbors. He wants you to be kind to them and do good to them.

Who were the Samaritans, and why didn't Jews like them?

Did God love the Samaritans, even though the Jews didn't?

66. IS THIS A BIBLE VERSE: "GOD HELPS THOSE WHO HELP THEMSELVES"?

\\\\\\\\\\\\\\\\\\\\\\\\\\\\

That *sounds* like a Bible verse. But it's actually not from the Bible. It comes from Aesop's Fables. Aesop lived in Greece about 2,600 years ago. He made up many fables. A fable is a story about an animal or a plant that acts and speaks like a human. A fable can also be about a force of nature (like the wind) or an imaginary creature. A fable ends with a short moral. A moral is a sentence that sums up the lesson of a story.

This moral—"God helps those who help themselves"—comes from the fable, *Hercules and the Waggoner*. A waggoner is a wagon driver. Long ago, they carried food and other goods to city markets. They were the truckers of the ancient world. One day, a waggoner was driving a heavy load down a muddy road. He came to a place where the mud was deep, and the wheels sank in it. The man whipped his horses, but it was no use. The wagon was stuck, and the poor horses couldn't pull it out.

The driver lay down in the wagon and cried out, "O Hercules the Strong, help me in my hour of need!" In Aesop's fable, the god Hercules showed up and looked at the situation. He saw that the driver wasn't willing to get down in the mud and push the wagon himself. He expected

Hercules to do it all for him.

Hercules became upset. He ordered, "Don't just lay there, man! Get up and put your shoulder to the wheel. The gods help those who help themselves." Centuries later, a Christian changed the words to "God helps those who help themselves." (Now you *also* know where the saying, "Put your shoulder to the wheel," comes from.)

There is some truth to this moral: God expects you to do what you *can* do to help yourself. In Paul's day, some lazy Christians quit their jobs and were mooching off other believers. Paul told them, "Work with your own hands, as we commanded you" (1 Thessalonians 4:11 NKJV). He added, "If anyone will not work, he will not eat" (2 Thessalonians 3:10 ICB).

But if you're talking about saving yourself by being a good person, then this saying is *not* scriptural. God saves those who can't save themselves— those who are weak and unable. "When we were utterly helpless, Christ came at just the right time and died for us sinners" (Romans 5:6 NLT).

Do even Aesop's fables have *some* wisdom in them?

When is this fable's lesson true? When is it not true?

67. WHY DO GROWN-UPS ARGUE ABOUT WHAT THE BIBLE SAYS?

\\\\\\\\\\\\\\\\\\\\\\\\\\\

Adults sometimes disagree about what the Bible says. A lot of the time, that's fine. As long as they agree on the important things, it's okay to disagree about small things. Here are some important things Christians should agree on: There is only one God. Jesus Christ is the Son of God. Jesus died for your sins and came back to life. Only Jesus can save you. You can't save yourself. The Bible is God's only true Word. You must love God with all your heart. You must love other people.

Many other things aren't that important. They are only people's opinions. They're not worth arguing about. Paul wrote:

> Welcome those who are weak in faith, but do not argue with them about their personal opinions. Some people's faith allows them to eat anything, but the person who is weak in the faith eats only vegetables. The person who will eat anything is not to despise the one who doesn't; while the one who eats only vegetables is not to pass judgment on the one who will eat anything; for God has accepted that person. (Romans 14:1–3 GNT)

Sometimes you must "agree to disagree." That

means you still love the other person, even when you disagree with them. If you can't change their mind, you wait for God to change their mind. You won't feel like *you* have to change the way they think.

However, some people are eager to argue, even over small things. It's often because they're proud. The Bible says: "Pride leads to arguments" (Proverbs 13:10 ICB). Arguing with people usually doesn't convince them that they're wrong. It just makes them mad.

What if you disagree about something important? You still shouldn't yell. Even when you disagree, gently explain your reasons. Don't quarrel. Even when they believe something untrue, be patient with them. The Bible says, "A servant of the Lord must not quarrel but must be kind to everyone, be able to teach, and be patient with difficult people. Gently instruct those who oppose the truth" (2 Timothy 2:24–25 NLT).

Yes, you are to be kind and patient and gentle with others, even if you think they're missing the truth. You may think it's very important to show them they're wrong. But losing your temper with them won't convince them.

Adults aren't the only ones who disagree about what the Bible says. Sometimes kids disagree too. Are you guilty of arguing?

- -

What is one of the main reasons people argue and quarrel?

When you disagree with someone, what are you supposed to do?

68. DO WE STILL NEED TO OBEY THE TEN COMMANDMENTS?

\\\\\\\\\\\\\\\\\\\\\\\\\\

Yes, you still need to obey the Ten Commandments. You don't need to keep all the many little laws of Moses. After all, Moses said Israelites had to kill animals to have their sins forgiven. Then they had to smear the animals' blood on people and things. This cleansed them. Now Christians are cleansed by the blood of Christ. But God's Ten Commands still apply. We still need them. Let's look at them closer and see.

In the first commandment, God said: "Worship no god but me" (Exodus 20:3 GNT). You certainly need to keep obeying *that* command. God still doesn't want people to worship other gods.

The second commandment is: "Do not make for yourselves images.... Do not bow down to any idol or worship it" (vv. 4–5). Does God now *want* you to make images and idols? Of course not. So you still need to obey that command too.

The third commandment is: "Do not use my name for evil purposes" (v. 7). God still doesn't want you to speak His name in an evil way.

The fourth commandment is: "Observe the Sabbath and keep it holy. You have six days in which to do your work, but the seventh day is a day of rest dedicated to me. On that day no one is to work" (vv. 8–10). Your body still needs one day of rest a week—whether Saturday or Sunday. That rule hasn't changed.

The fifth commandment is: "Respect your father and your mother" (v. 12). God still wants Christians to respect their parents.

The sixth commandment is: "Do not commit murder" (v. 13). Murder is still a wicked idea.

The seventh commandment is: "Do not commit adultery" (v. 14). God wants husbands and wives to live their lives together and love each other faithfully.

The eighth commandment is: "Do not steal" (v. 15). Stealing is selfish and hurtful, so you still shouldn't steal.

The ninth commandment is: "Do not accuse anyone falsely" (v. 16). This law is still in effect too.

The tenth commandment is: "Do not desire another man's house. . .or anything else that he owns" (v. 17). Wanting someone else's things is still wrong. Because then you might try to steal them. So don't desire others' belongings.

As you can see, the Ten Commandments are still very important. And Christians should still obey them.

Why do some people think you don't need to obey the Ten Commandments?

Which of the Ten Commandments is it now okay to ignore?

69. WHY DO CHRISTIANS SOMETIMES DO BAD THINGS?

\\\\\\\\\\\\\\\\\\\\\\\\\\\\\

You may sometimes hear a Christian man use a curse word when he's angry—or when he injures himself. Or maybe he takes a pen that doesn't belong to him. Or you may hear a Christian lady say something that isn't true. And you wonder, "Don't they know they're not supposed to do that?" Yes, they probably know. So why do they do it?

Well, you may think once someone is a Christian, they never sin again. You may be tempted to judge them. When a follower of Jesus disobeys Him, it's natural to think, "That's a sin!" Or, if a believer stumbles and does something wrong, you may think they're a hypocrite. Some people *are* hypocrites—but it's usually not *your* place to judge if someone is or not.

Jesus said, "Do not judge others, so that God will not judge you, for God will judge you in the same way you judge others, and he will apply to you the same rules you apply to others" (Matthew 7:1–2 GNT).

And remember, Christians are still human. And human beings aren't perfect. The apostle John told Christians not to sin. But he also realized that everyone sins from time to time. He wrote: "I am writing this to you, my children, so that you will *not sin*; but if anyone *does* sin, we have someone who pleads with the Father on our behalf—Jesus Christ." John also said, "But if we confess our sins to God, he will. . .forgive us our sins and purify us from all our wrongdoing" (1 John 2:1; 1:9 GNT, emphasis added).

If you see an adult doing something wrong, you can mention it to them. But speak to them respectfully. Maybe they're doing it without thinking. Maybe when you remind them, they'll apologize and make things right. Or maybe they weren't doing anything wrong. Maybe you just didn't know all the facts. You may never know unless you speak up. . .respectfully.

If you see someone doing something *seriously* bad, talk to an adult whom you trust. Tell them what's happening. Sometimes even Christians are tempted to sin in big ways, and do things that are very wrong. Maybe they're stealing money, or doing drugs, or hurting themselves or others. They need help, but you're probably not the person who can best give them help. They need help from strong Christian adults to stop what they're doing (see Galatians 6:1).

Why is it usually *not* good to criticize and judge others?

When *should* you speak up about someone's bad behavior?

70. WHY DO WE GO TO CHURCH ON SUNDAY?

\\\\\\\\\\\\\\\\\\\\\\\\\\\\

Ever since they left Egypt, the Jews honored God on the Sabbath (Saturday) by resting from their work. They also prayed and thought about God and His Word. After they settled in Israel, the Jews built a temple for God in Jerusalem. But most Jews didn't go there on the Sabbath. They didn't live in Jerusalem. They lived in cities and small towns and villages all over Israel.

Later, the Babylonians took the Jews far away to Babylon. The Jews in Babylon began gathering on the Sabbath to read the Bible and to pray. It was hard to be faithful to God in a land that worshipped idols. So the Jews also gathered to encourage one another to stay true. They began meeting in special buildings. Today, we call these buildings synagogues.

Later, the Jews returned to Israel and rebuilt the temple. They also began building synagogues in every city and town of Israel. In Jesus' day, all faithful Jews attended a synagogue on the Sabbath.

At first, Jews who became Christians kept going to synagogues. But many of them were kicked out because they believed in Jesus (see John 9:22; 12:42). So they began meeting in homes. Paul often talked about churches (groups of believers) that met in someone's home (see Romans 16:5;

Colossians 4:15; Philemon 1:1–2).

Also, most Christians began meeting on Sunday, not Saturday. This was because God had raised Jesus to life on a Sunday (Mark 16:2). To the Jews, Saturday was the last day of the week. Sunday was the first day of the week. That's why the Bible talks about Christians meeting and giving money to God on "the first day of the week" (Acts 20:7; 1 Corinthians 16:2). But some Christians go to church on Saturday.

Some people didn't think it was important to gather. They said, "I don't need to go to a meeting on Sunday to be a Christian." But a Christian leader wrote, "Let us not give up the habit of meeting together, as some are doing. Instead, let us encourage one another all the more, since you see that the Day of the Lord is coming nearer" (Hebrews 10:25 GNT).

Christians today still meet to encourage one another to be true to God. They also meet to sing worship songs to God. And they listen to pastors preach a sermon from the Bible. It's also a good time to give money to God. There are lots of good reasons to go to church.

What does your church do during its meetings once a week?

How can you encourage other Christians at church?

71. WHY DO WE SING SONGS IN CHURCH AND PRAISE GOD?

\\\\\\\\\\\\\\\\\\\\\\\\\

The Psalms say again and again that people should praise God. They say: "Praise the Lord! Praise the Lord, my soul! I will praise him as long as I live; I will sing to my God all my life" (Psalm 146:1–2 GNT). "Praise the Lord! It is good to sing praise to our God; it is pleasant and right to praise him" (Psalm 147:1 GNT). "Let them all praise the name of the Lord! His name is greater than all others; his glory is above earth and heaven" (Psalm 148:13 GNT).

Why do the Psalms say this so often? Why does God enjoy hearing people praise Him so much? Actually, the reason Christians should praise the Lord is because the wonderful things they say about Him are *true*. His name *is* truly greater than all others. His glory really *is* greater than the glory of heaven and earth. You're not just saying nice things about God to make Him feel good. Honestly, He doesn't need it.

Praising God also helps you understand how great and wonderful and powerful He is. When you realize these things, it helps you look to Him for the answers to your problems. It helps you to trust Him in your time of need. So when you take time to pray, it's good to first worship God. God enjoys hearing sincere praise. But as you can see, it does you a lot of good too.

You would get bored if you simply said, "Praise God!" over and over again. And you might not be able to think of so many different things to praise Him for. So that's why people sing songs of praise. It's easy to praise God with singing. And it sounds beautiful!

However, praising God is *not* the most important thing. Jesus said, "'Love the Lord your God with all your heart, with all your soul, and with all your mind.' This is the greatest and the most important commandment" (Matthew 22:37–38 GNT). You must truly love God. The prophet Isaiah talked about people who honored God with their words, but their hearts were far from Him. God said, "It is no use for them to worship me" (Matthew 15:9 GNT).

You may notice that very young children really don't get into worship in church. They'd rather color pictures or read a book. But remember, they're little. They don't know any better. As they grow up, they'll become more interested in God.

What is your favorite praise and worship song?

Why do you like it?

How does praising God help you?

72. WHY DO WE GIVE MONEY TO GOD?

\\\\\\\\\\\\\\\\\\\\\\\

Christians usually give money to God by giving to their church. You give money for lots of good reasons. Let's think about some of those reasons. First: the church needs money to pay for the building you meet in. It costs money to pay for the heat and lights. You wouldn't want to be *without* them, would you?

And don't forget your pastors and church secretaries. Your pastor and youth pastor and children's pastor work hard taking care of people. They feed them God's Word. They talk to people who have problems. They encourage them. But remember: pastors also need money to pay their bills and buy food. "Elders who do their work well should be respected and paid well, especially those who work hard at both preaching and teaching" (1 Timothy 5:17 NLT).

Your church also needs money for missionaries. "How can they believe if they have not heard the message? And how can they hear if the message is not proclaimed? And how can the message be proclaimed if the messengers are not sent out?" (Romans 10:14–15 GNT). So your church needs to send out missionaries. It costs a lot of money to send a family to another country. And they will have bills to pay every month, like everyone else.

Your church also needs money to help people who are poor. Or a family may need a bit of help if their father loses his job. Peter and James reminded Paul: "They asked us to. . .remember to help the poor" (Galatians 2:10 ICB).

So give to God! He will *bless* you for giving. "Give to others, and God will give to you. Indeed, you will receive a full measure, a generous helping, poured into your hands—all that you can hold. The measure you use for others is the one that God will use for you" (Luke 6:38 GNT).

Some people believe that they should tithe to their church. To tithe means to faithfully give 10 percent of your income. The Bible says, "Bring the full amount of your tithes to the Temple" (Malachi 3:10 GNT). Other Christians don't believe that Christians need to tithe because Jesus and the apostles didn't say to. But Jesus did talk a lot about giving generously. "You should each give, then, as you have decided, not with regret or out of a sense of duty; for God loves the one who gives gladly" (2 Corinthians 9:7 GNT).

What does your church do with the money you give to them?

What are different ways God might bless you for giving to Him?

73. WHY DO I HAVE TO READ THE BIBLE EVERY DAY?

\\\\\\\\\\\\\\\\\\\\\\\\\\

Some parents make their children read a chapter from the Bible every day. Are those kids ever fortunate! They're learning the most valuable stuff they could possibly learn! Your parents may make *you* read one or two chapters from the Bible every day. You might not think it's so enjoyable—especially if they make you read before watching TV or playing video games. It may sometimes feel like homework.

Also, you may not find parts of the Bible very exciting—like the chapters in Leviticus that talk about mold growing on walls. But many other parts of scripture are *very* interesting. And most important, they give you wisdom and tell you how to live. Some chapters like Psalm 23, John 15, and 1 Corinthians 13 are very important. In fact, it's good to read them often.

It's a wonderful thing if you read your Bible every day. You can learn so much! The reason many Christians make big mistakes is because they don't *know* what the Bible says. They simply have no idea. They've never opened a Bible and read it. So they often do wrong things. Jesus told some people, "You don't understand because you don't know what the Scriptures say" (Matthew 22:29 ICB).

Jesus often asked the religious people questions like, "Didn't you ever read this in the Scriptures?" (Matthew 21:42 NLT). They read it all right, but they didn't clue in. Some people today read their Bible, but they read it too fast. They don't slow down and think about what it's saying.

Or even if they *do* understand it, they don't take the next step. They don't try to see how it applies to their life. How do they miss the lessons? Simple. They're not really paying attention. No wonder they soon forget them. No wonder Jesus asks, "Didn't you ever read this in the scriptures?"

It's important to read a translation of the Bible you can understand. For example, the King James Version is a wonderful translation. But it's four hundred years old. It's often very difficult to follow. Some of the best Bibles for your age are the Good News Translation, the New Living Translation, or the International Children's Bible. Those are the Bibles we quote from the most in this book (see Nehemiah 8:8).

So read the scriptures today. Start by reading Genesis and Exodus. Then skip ahead to the New Testament. Read what Jesus and His disciples taught.

- -

Why is it so important to read your Bible?

Why do you need to understand how God's
  Word applies to your life?

74. WHY DO I HAVE TO MEMORIZE VERSES FROM THE BIBLE?

\\\\\\\\\\\\\\\\\\\\\\\\\

Count yourself blessed if your parents make you memorize Bible verses. God told parents, "Always remember these commands I give you today. Teach them to your children" (Deuteronomy 6:6–7 ICB). But why is it good to memorize Bible verses? Here are some things memorizing does for you:

(1) It helps you connect to Jesus. "Keep your roots deep in him and have your lives built on him. Be strong in the faith" (Colossians 2:7 ICB). Jesus said, "Those who accept my commandments and obey them are the ones who love me" (John 14:21 NLT). But it's difficult to obey Him if you don't know what He said.

(2) It helps you make decisions. If you memorize verses they can guide you to make wise choices. Jesus said about the Holy Spirit: "He will cause you to remember all the things I told you" (John 14:26 ICB). But you need to *know* Jesus' words before the Spirit can remind you of them.

(3) It helps you avoid sin. "I have taken your words to heart so I would not sin against you" (Psalm 119:11 ICB). Jesus quoted the Word of God to the devil when he tempted Jesus to disobey God (see Matthew 4:1–10). If you know the Bible says not to do something, you can stay away from it.

(4) It gets rid of confusion. If you don't know what the Bible says, people can trick you. Jesus told the religious leaders, "You are in error because you do not know the Scriptures" (Matthew 22:29 NIV). But if you know God's Word, you "will not be influenced by every new teaching we hear" (Ephesians 4:14 ICB).

(5) It helps you tell others about Jesus. If you memorize verses like Romans 3:23; 6:23, and John 3:16, you can quote them to people. First Peter 3:15 (NIV) says, "Always be prepared to give an answer to everyone who asks you to give the reason for the hope that you have."

(6) It protects you from the devil. Ephesians 6:16 (ICB) says, "And also use the shield of faith. With that you can stop all the burning arrows of the Evil One." How do you get the shield of faith? Romans 10:17 (ICB) says, "So faith comes from hearing the Good News. . .about Christ."

(7) It gives you spiritual authority. God had made promises to Jacob down through the years. When he faced danger, Jacob quoted those promises back to God (see Genesis 32:9–12).

What are several good reasons to memorize Bible verses?

How many Bible verses can you quote?

75. WHY DO KIDS ALWAYS HAVE TO OBEY THEIR PARENTS?

\\\\\\\\\\\\\\\\\\\\\\\\\

The Ten Commandments are very important laws. And one of them says, "Honor your father and mother. Then you will live a long, full life in the land the LORD your God is giving you" (Exodus 20:12 NLT). How do you honor your parents? The main way you do that is by obeying them. The apostle Paul said: "Children, obey your parents because you belong to the Lord, for this is the right thing to do" (Ephesians 6:1 NLT).

You may wonder why you should *always* obey your parents. Sure, you understand the obvious reason: they're older than you. They have learned many things during their lives. You won't always understand why they tell you to do something, or not to do something. But you know that they know more than you do.

In fact, that's why you are to honor *all* older men and women. Moses said, "Show respect for old people and honor them" (Leviticus 19:32 GNT).

But that's not the only reason. Another reason is that your mom and dad love you very much and want you to be healthy and safe. When they give you instructions, it's for your own good. So you're taking care of yourself by obeying them.

Another way to honor your parents is to offer

them your chair to sit in when they enter a room. It's also polite to let them serve their food before you. Of course, your parents may put *your* needs before theirs and serve *you* first. Sometimes you have to let them do that. But when you have a chance to honor your parents, do it.

What do you do when you think your parents are wrong? Or what do you do if you think they're being unfair? You might be tempted to whine and complain, or sulk until they give you what you want. But you should obey them instead. You can respectfully ask them about their decision. But if they don't change their minds, you should still obey them.

Sometimes when parents become very old, they don't always make the best decisions anymore. But you shouldn't despise them. To "despise" someone means to look down on him or her and not take them seriously. Solomon wrote "Listen to your father, who gave you life, and don't despise your mother when she is old" (Proverbs 23:22 NLT). And remember. Your parents probably aren't "very" old yet. So they most likely *are* making the best decisions. So respect them.

How often should you show respect to your parents?

What did God say would happen if you honored your parents?

76. DOES GOD PROMISE TO BLESS ME IF I'M GOOD?

\\\\\\\\\\\\\\\\\\\\\\\\\\\\

Yes, He does! Jesus promised that God would bless you for several reasons. For example, He said, "It is more blessed to give than to receive" (Acts 20:35 NIV). And He promised, "Give, and you will receive. . . . The way you give to others is the way God will give to you" (Luke 6:38 ICB). God blesses you for giving money to church. He also blesses you for giving to the poor. God blesses you when you give your time to help others. God blesses you for showing love and kindness to people.

What does "bless" mean? It means that when you please God, He looks on you with favor. Then, because He favors you, He makes good things happen in your life. Sometimes they won't seem like big miracles. But they are God's work, just the same.

And *how* does God bless you? Some people think if they give money, that God will turn around and bless them with lots *more* money. Sometimes He does things that way. But that isn't always the way God rewards you. Sometimes He blesses you by protecting you from accidents. Sometimes He blesses you with good health. God blesses you lots of different ways.

But remember, just because God promises to

bless you, doesn't mean you'll never have problems. It doesn't mean you'll never lose things. It doesn't mean you'll never get sick. Some of your blessings will come right now in this life, and that's good. But many blessings will only come to you in heaven.

Jesus said, "God blesses you who are poor, for the Kingdom of God is yours. God blesses you who are hungry now, for you will be satisfied. God blesses you who weep now, for in due time you will laugh. What blessings await you when people hate you and exclude you and mock you and curse you as evil because you follow the Son of Man. When that happens, be happy! Yes, leap for joy! For a great reward awaits you in heaven" (Luke 6:20–23 NLT).

In all the cases above, people still suffered in this life. They continued to be poor. They continued to be hungry. They continued to weep. They continued to be persecuted. But when they got to heaven, all that ended. Then they were greatly blessed. You won't receive all your rewards in *this* life. But you will definitely be rewarded in heaven.

What are the different ways that God blesses you?

Why doesn't God give you all your blessings now in *this* life?

77. DOES GOD STILL SPEAK TO PEOPLE THROUGH DREAMS TODAY?

\\\\\\\\\\\\\\\\\\\\\\\\\\

God is still busy doing the same thing He's always done. In Bible days, He sometimes spoke to people in their dreams. For example, he spoke to Jacob's son, Joseph, to Pharaoh, and to Mary's husband, Joseph (see Genesis 37:5–10; 41:1–7; Matthew 1:20–21; 2:13, 19–20). And God can still speak to people through dreams today.

But most of the time, even in Bible days, people's dreams weren't messages from God. They were just dreams. Whatever they were busy doing or thinking about all day long, usually made its way into their dreams. They chewed on thoughts, swallowed them deep into their minds, then burped them up again later.

It's the same today. When you think about something a lot during the day, you often dream about it at night. That's usually why people have nightmares. They watch scary movies or TV shows, or they read strange books. Then those pictures and sounds come back to them while they sleep. So if you often have nightmares, check what you're reading and watching. "Be careful how you think; your life is shaped by your thoughts" (Proverbs 4:23 GNT).

Many people claim that their dreams are messages from God. But God warned about false prophets who said, "I have had a dream! I have had a dream!!" God said these dreams were only "their own wishful thinking" (Jeremiah 23:25–26 ICB). Their dreams came from their own minds, not from God.

One of the biggest causes of dreams is worry. The Bible says: "Bad dreams come from too much worrying" (Ecclesiastes 5:3 ICB). If you worry about something, it may come to you in a dream. For example, say you're worried about a bully at school. You may have a dream that a monster is chasing you. You try running away, but you can't run. This isn't a message from God. But it *may* be a message from your brain. Your mind may be telling you, "I'm afraid of the bully. I feel like I can't get away from him."

The solution to nightmares is usually simple. Often you have bad dreams because you forgot to pray before you went to bed. You'd be surprised how often you simply need to pray, "Lord, please give me sweet dreams tonight."

Back to the original question: "Does God still speak to people through dreams today?" Sometimes He does. If you get a clear message in a dream, tell it to your parents. See what they think it means.

Are most dreams messages from God? If not, what are they?

What can you do to keep from having nightmares?

78. WHY DO I HAVE TO PRAY IF GOD ALREADY KNOWS WHAT I NEED?

\\\\\\\\\\\\\\\\\\\\\\\\

Jesus said, "When you pray, do not use a lot of meaningless words, as the pagans do, who think that their gods will hear them because their prayers are long. Your Father already knows what you need before you ask him" (Matthew 6:7–8 GNT). Another Bible says it this way: "When you pray, don't babble on and on as the Gentiles do. They think their prayers are answered merely by repeating their words again and again. Don't be like them, for your Father knows exactly what you need even before you ask him!" (Matthew 6:7–8 NLT).

Many people ask, "Why do I have to pray at all if God already knows what I need?" Well, Jesus didn't say, "Don't pray at all." He said don't repeat the *same* words again and again. Don't say a lot of fluffy words just to make your prayers last longer.

Keep your prayers simple. Ask for what you need and then finish. Don't repeat yourself again and again in the same prayer. If you do, you act like God has trouble hearing. God has no problem hearing. And don't think of clever new ways to say the same old thing. God isn't impressed by long, fancy prayers.

But you *can* mention the same need when you

pray later in the day—or the next day. If God hasn't answered yet, and you still need it, then pray about it again. "Jesus told his disciples a parable to teach them that they should always pray and never become discouraged" (Luke 18:1 GNT). Paul told Timothy, "I remember you always in my prayers night and day" (2 Timothy 1:3 GNT). And Paul wrote, "Never stop praying" (1 Thessalonians 5:17 ICB).

And remember: you need to pray more over a big problem than a little one. The Bible says that when Peter was arrested and kept in prison, the church made "constant prayer" to God for him (Acts 12:5 NKJV). "Constant prayer" means they continued to pray without stopping. They kept praying because their hearts were overflowing with emotion.

There's another reason God wants you to pray for what you need. Every time you pray to God, it reminds you that He is God. It reminds you that you depend on Him. If you never prayed, how would you know it was *God* who supplied your needs? You might think things just happened on their own. So don't be lazy. Pray today!

Why does God like short, sincere prayers better than fat, fluffy prayers?

When is it okay to pray about the same need again?

79. WHY DOESN'T GOD ANSWER ALL MY PRAYERS?

\\\\\\\\\\\\\\\\\\\\\\\

God doesn't answer all your prayers because some of them aren't His will. You may be asking for something He doesn't want you to have. God knows exactly what you need. He knows what you need even better than you do. You might be praying for Him to do something, when you should actually be praying for something else. That's why it's good to pray, "If it's Your will, give me this" or "If it's Your will, let this happen." Even Jesus prayed, "Not My will, but Yours, be done" (Luke 22:42 NKJV).

So you must ask for something that He wants you to have. The apostle John wrote, "We have courage in God's presence, because we are sure that he hears us if we ask him for anything that is according to his will. . . . And since we know this is true, we know also that he gives us what we ask from him" (1 John 5:14–15 GNT).

Many Christians don't really want God's will. They only want God's will if it's easy and comfortable. But sometimes God's will is hard or uncomfortable. Many Christians pray for selfish things. No wonder God doesn't answer their prayers. Here are some more thoughts to help you get answers to your prayers:

You must have *faith* that God will answer you.

"When you pray and ask for something, believe that you have received it, and you will be given whatever you ask for" (Mark 11:24 GNT). If you don't believe God can answer your prayers, there's no point in praying. But some people read Mark 11:24 all by itself. They think if they only have enough faith, God will give them *whatever* they want. This isn't true.

You must also be obedient to God. The apostle John wrote, "We receive from him whatever we ask, because we obey his commands and do what pleases him" (1 John 3:22 GNT). If you're doing something that *doesn't* please God, you won't have much faith that He will answer your prayers.

Don't be discouraged if it takes a long time to get answers to prayer. Don't give up and think that God doesn't care. Don't think He isn't going to answer you. God actually *is* answering many prayers—even though it seems like He's not. It's just taking a while for Him to get all the pieces in place. But in God's timing, it will happen.

What three things do you need to do to get answers to prayer?

Why should you not give up praying if the answers take a long time?

80. WHY DO I NEED TO SAY I'M SORRY TO PEOPLE?

\\\\\\\\\\\\\\\\\\\\\\\\

The first thing to know is that God loves you very much. He knows every time you're sad or discouraged. He sees your tears. He feels your sorrow when someone has done wrong to you. He cares about your feelings. So He wants them to be sorry that they hurt you. He wants them to apologize. Does that make sense? Of course it does! "God is love" (1 John 4:8 NLT) and He loves *you*!

But remember: God loves your brother or sister as much as He loves you. He loves your friends and neighbors. He cares about how they feel too. And He wants *you* to love them and care about their feelings. That's why one of the greatest commandments of all is: "Love your neighbor as you love yourself" (Matthew 22:39 ICB). You care when others hurt you, don't you? You care when someone hurts your brother or sister, don't you? Well, you should also care if *you* have hurt them.

The apostle Peter put it perfectly. He said: "Finally, all of you should be of one mind. Sympathize with each other. Love each other as brothers and sisters. Be tenderhearted, and keep a humble attitude" (1 Peter 3:8 NLT). You should have sympathy for others. You should have a caring, tender heart toward them.

But if you're still angry with them, it can be

very hard to say you're sorry. When your parents tell you to apologize to someone, you may not feel like it. Even if you *know* you did wrong to that person. There's no sense in saying you're sorry if you still want to hurt someone. They'll know you're *not* sorry. They'll know you still want to cause them pain. Before you say you're sorry, you need to *be* sorry. You need to know that you've done wrong, and feel bad about it.

But a lot of times, your pride will stop you. You know you've done wrong, but you don't want to say "I'm sorry" out loud. Very often, pride stops people from apologizing. That's when you should remember what Peter said: "Be tenderhearted, and keep a humble attitude" (1 Peter 3:8 NLT). If you're very proud, you'll never apologize. It's much better to be humble.

Swallow your pride and apologize to the person you hurt. You'll start feeling better very quickly. And so will the other person. It might even help if you hug them.

Why does God want you to care about other people's feelings?

What's the thing that often stops you from apologizing?

81. WHY DOES GOD LET KIDS BE SO MEAN?

\\\\\\\\\\\\\\\\\\\\\\

Some kids are mean because they're treated badly at home. Maybe someone has been mean to them before. Or someone is being mean to them now. So they become angry. Then they take out their anger on other kids. But some kids are mean for no reason. They're just bullies. They make up their mind to be miserable to others. They think it's fun to torment smaller kids.

You might ask, "Why does God *let* kids be so mean?" The God who created the entire universe can do anything. So you may ask: "If God *has* the power to solve problems and stop suffering, why doesn't He?"

One of the main reasons is that, although God *can* do anything, He has limited Himself by giving humans free will. This is why you can choose what you *will* or will *not* do. The problem is that people often choose to do selfish things— and choose not to do good. God doesn't usually stop you from making wrong choices. If He did, He'd be taking away your free will. Some people wish that He would. But then everyone would be mindless robots.

Because people have free will, their bad choices cause pain in the world. This is why there is gossiping, stealing, bullying, murders, and wars.

Selfish people cause pain. The wicked cause suffering. And God is *not* okay with that. The Bible tells us, "God is angry with the wicked every day" (Psalm 7:11 NKJV). God will stop them one day. He says, "I, the LORD, will punish the world for its evil and the wicked for their sin" (Isaiah 13:11 NLT). He will judge them for the wrong choices they make. God shows them mercy now. But if they refuse to change, one day they'll suffer for it.

But remember: Jesus can change people's lives. Many selfish bullies have been changed when they believed in Jesus. His Spirit came into their lives and saved them. "This means that anyone who belongs to Christ has become a new person. The old life is gone; a new life has begun!" (2 Corinthians 5:17 NLT). So pray that they will turn to God and let Him change them.

In the meantime, if they keep on bullying you, tell an adult. Tell your parents or tell a teacher. Don't just let them keep tormenting you. (See the answer to the question, "Why do I have to let bullies slap me around?" on page 169.)

Why doesn't God change all the bad people immediately?

What is "free will"? Are you glad God gave it to you?

82. DO I HAVE TO FORGIVE EVERYONE WHO HURTS ME?

\\\\\\\\\\\\\\\\\\\\\\\\

It hurts when someone does something wrong to you. Jesus knows that. He also knows that it causes pain when a friend says bad things about you. He knows because people hurt *Him*. People said bad things about *Him*. What did Jesus do when this happened? He forgave them. He even forgave those who spat on Him, whipped Him, and nailed Him to a cross. As He was dying on the cross, He said, "Father, forgive them, for they don't know what they are doing" (Luke 23:34 NLT).

Jesus understands what you're going through. The Bible says, "For our high priest is able to understand our weaknesses. He was tempted in every way that we are, but he did not sin" (Hebrews 4:15 ICB). If Jesus was "tempted in every way that we are," that means He was tempted to ask God to judge people who hurt Him. He was tempted to hold a grudge against them. But He didn't. He forgave them.

Jesus taught His disciples, "When you are praying, first forgive anyone you are holding a grudge against, so that your Father in heaven will forgive your sins, too" (Mark 11:25 NLT). If you don't forgive others, your heavenly Father won't forgive your sins. That's a scary thought. It shows how important forgiveness is to God.

Moses wrote: "Do not seek revenge or bear a grudge against anyone among your people, but love your neighbor as yourself" (Leviticus 19:18 NIV). If you don't forgive someone, you'll try to take revenge on them. You'll try to hurt them the way they hurt you. Even if you don't seek revenge, you'll hold a grudge.

What is a grudge? It's secret hatred. When you hold grudges against people, you may not hurt them physically, but you'll speak bad things about them all the time. You'll seek to hurt them other ways. Think of it like this: if revenge is an open, burning fire, a grudge is a smoldering, smoking fire. It may not burn like a flame, but it can still hurt people. And that's wrong.

King Solomon wrote, "It is foolish to harbor a grudge" (Ecclesiastes 7:9 GNT). Why is it foolish? Because often it causes more damage to *you* than it does to the person you hate. It's burning inside you. So refuse to hold a grudge. Let the pain go. Forgive those who have hurt you. You'll be glad you did.

What happens if you don't forgive someone who hurt you?

What is a grudge? What kind of damage can it cause?

83. WHY DO I HAVE TO LET BULLIES SLAP ME AROUND?

\\\\\\\\\\\\\\\\\\\\\\\\

Jesus said, "You have heard that it was said, 'An eye for an eye, and a tooth for a tooth.' But now I tell you: do not take revenge on someone who wrongs you. If anyone slaps you on the right cheek, let him slap your left cheek too" (Matthew 5:38–39 GNT). Jesus had a good reason for saying this. But some people think He meant that if bullies attack you, you should just let them slap you around all day long. It *doesn't* mean that.

When I was a boy, I saw two bullies inside my school doors. One was holding a boy so he couldn't move. The other bully drew on his face with a felt marker. The boy ran home, crying. Then the bullies attacked me. But I put up a fight, so they backed off. Then I went to the school office and told the secretary what they were doing. The bullies got in trouble. Later they accused me, saying, "You squealed on us!" But I told them they shouldn't have been picking on people. The bullies didn't try that again.

You may think that if bullies knock your books on the floor, you should just let them do it. Or if they try to take your lunch money, you should let them take it. But Jesus said, "When a strong man with many weapons guards his own house, then the things in his house are safe" (Luke 11:21 ICB).

What did Jesus mean then? Well, remember that He *first* said, "Do not take revenge on someone who wrongs you." You should stand up for your rights and defend yourself. But if you're stronger—or if there are more kids on your side—don't try to do evil back to the bullies. Solomon wrote: "Don't say, 'Now I can pay them back for what they've done to me! I'll get even with them!' " (Proverbs 24:29 NLT).

In Jesus' day—just like today—if someone slaps your face, they aren't really trying to *hurt* you. If they were trying to hurt you, they would punch you instead. A slap is mostly an insult. Jesus meant you aren't supposed to insult them back. The Bible says, "Do not do wrong to a person to pay him back for doing wrong to you. Or do not insult someone to pay him back for insulting you. But ask God to bless that person. Do this, because you yourselves were called to receive a blessing" (1 Peter 3:9 ICB).

Why shouldn't you insult someone back if they insult you?

What should you do instead of seeking revenge?

84. WHY DO I HAVE TO LOVE MY ENEMIES?

\\\\\\\\\\\\\\\\\\\\\\\

Many Christians don't know why Jesus said, "Love your enemies. Do good to those who hate you. Ask God to bless those who say bad things to you. Pray for those who are cruel to you" (Luke 6:27–28 ICB). They don't love their enemies. And they don't understand why they should. They think that the only reason Jesus had enough love to do that was because He was the Son of God. But they don't think He really expects *them* to love *their* enemies. So they have no idea why He told them to.

But Jesus really meant it. He didn't just say it once in this chapter. He said it twice. A few verses later, He repeated, "So love your enemies. Do good to them. . . . If you do these things, you will have a great reward. You will be sons of the Most High God. Yes, because God is kind even to people who are ungrateful and full of sin" (Luke 6:35 ICB).

You should love people who are unthankful. And you should even love people who act evil. Why? Because God loves them. So if you belong to God, you'll love like He loves. It proves that you're His child. It proves that you know Him. "But anyone who does not love does not know God, for God is love" (1 John 4:8 NLT).

But just because you love people doesn't mean that you should love what they *do*. What if they're doing evil things? The Bible commands. "People who love the Lord should hate evil" (Psalm 97:10 ICB). God wants unthankful people to be thankful. He doesn't like it when they keep taking things without being grateful. And God wants evil people to be good. He doesn't like it when they keep hurting people. But for now, He shows mercy to them.

In the end of the world, God will judge all selfish and evil people. Then they will suffer if they lived their lives selfishly. They will be punished if they never repented. But for now, He gives them many chances to change.

How can you love them even if what they do makes you angry? You must let go of your anger and forgive them. Sometimes it will be very difficult to do this. But remember what Jesus prayed about His enemies. They had made Pilate crucify Him. But even as He was suffering and dying on the cross, Jesus said, "Forgive them, Father! They don't know what they are doing" (Luke 23:34 GNT).

Ask God to help you love your enemies today.

Are you able to love your enemies? Why or why not?

Why don't you need to love the things they're *doing*?

85. WHY DO CHRISTIANS NEED TO WITNESS TO OTHERS ABOUT JESUS?

\\\\\\\\\\\\\\\\\\\\\\\\\\

People need to believe in Jesus to be saved. And before they can believe, they need to hear about Him. So someone has to tell them. And who will tell them if not Christians? Jesus said, "Go into all the world and preach the Good News to everyone" (Mark 16:15 NLT). What good news? The good news that Jesus can save them and help them every day.

But often people aren't convinced by just hearing words. They want to watch you first to see if it works in *your* life. Jesus said, "People don't hide a light under a bowl. They put the light on a lampstand. Then the light shines for all the people in the house. In the same way, you should be a light for other people. Live so that they will see the good things you do. Live so that they will praise your Father in heaven" (Matthew 5:15–16 ICB).

Don't worry. This doesn't mean you have to be perfect and never make mistakes. But Christians are supposed to be honest. So they should see you return things that aren't yours. Christians are supposed to be kind. They should hear you say kind things. Christians are supposed to be forgiving. They should see you forgive someone who has hurt you. If you offend or hurt them, they should hear you apologize.

This doesn't mean you must put on a show of "being good." Don't do that! You'll get tired of that really quick. Just try to obey Jesus and do the things that please Him—all the time. After a while, people will notice. You may not even know when they're looking. The Bible says, "Do this not only when they are watching you, because you want to gain their approval; but with all your heart do what God wants" (Ephesians 6:6 GNT).

You should 'witness' to others with your words. But first of all, your *life* should witness to them. Your life should be an example of how Jesus helps you be honest, be kind, and be forgiving. When you talk to them about Jesus, they should know that He works for you.

Jesus said, "But when the Holy Spirit comes upon you, you will be filled with power, and you will be witnesses for me" (Acts 1:8 GNT). How do you get the Holy Spirit's power in your life? Take time to pray at the beginning of every day. Ask Him to help you. He will!

- -

What ways can your life "shine like a light" for Jesus?

Why do people want to first check out if Jesus works for *your* life?

86. WHY ARE THERE WARS?

\\\\\\\\\\\\\\\\\\\

As you already learned, soldiers are serving God when they protect their country. So make sure you honor the men and women of your military. Their job is dangerous. They sometimes lose their lives. Or they're badly wounded. Then they live for many years with their wounds. So you should respect them for their courage and sacrifices.

However, not all rulers send their soldiers to war for good reasons. Some rulers are greedy. They want the land, oil, or water that belongs to another country. Or they want revenge because of something the other nation did in the past. So they send their army into the other country. The Bible says, "What is causing the quarrels and fights among you? Don't they come from the evil desires at war within you? You want what you don't have, so you scheme and kill to get it. You are jealous of what others have. . .so you fight and wage war to take it away from them" (James 4:1–2 NLT).

The United Nations (UN) often sends soldiers from many countries into war zones. They go between two armies and keep them apart. That way the armies don't fight. Sometimes a country is divided and people inside the country are fighting one another. This is called a civil war. The UN soldiers then go into the country and keep the peace. It's often a very difficult job.

Why do countries have civil wars? Often it's

because some people in the country are one race, and other people are another race. So they hate each other. In ancient Israel, the Jews and the Samaritans hated each other. They tried to have nothing to do with each other. "Jews refuse to have anything to do with Samaritans" (John 4:9 NLT). At times, they got angry with each other and had battles. Some countries have civil wars because their people have different languages, different religions, or different politics.

Terrorists are filled with hatred for others. They do violent things to make people afraid. They think it will make God happy if they kill many people. They don't know God at all. They don't know that "God is love" (1 John 4:8 NIV).

Wars cause many problems. When armies are fighting, farmers can't grow food. They can't plant or harvest crops. Then the people starve. Nearly 870 million people around the world go to bed hungry every night. And 15 million children die of starvation every year. Much of this is because of wars. What a terrible thing wars are!

Are some soldiers doing a good thing by
   fighting in a war?

Are other soldiers fighting selfish wars?
   What makes these wars selfish?

87. WHEN WILL GOD FIX ALL THE WORLD'S PROBLEMS?

\\\\\\\\\\\\\\\\\\\\\\

This world we live in is a big, beautiful place, full of many wonderful things. In this country, you can enjoy wide oceans, cool forests, awesome geysers, and magnificent animals. But sad to say, people have wrecked much of this world. Much of the earth is now polluted. In many parts of India and China, the air is not good to breathe. Many of earth's rivers are so dirty you can't drink the water. The earth's coral reefs are dying. In the past, there were many tigers, rhinos, and gorillas. Now there are only a few left. It would be very sad if this world was completely destroyed. But that is what is happening. The Bible warns that this will happen. "A third of the sea was turned into blood, a third of the living creatures in the sea died . . . A third of the water turned bitter, and many people died from drinking the water, because it had turned bitter" (Revelation 8:8, 11 GNT). Then things will get even worse. One day, every living thing in the oceans will die (Revelation 16:3 GNT).

This sounds very gloomy, doesn't it? It would be very sad if that was the end, and nothing could ever change it. But there is wonderful news: after Jesus returns, God is going to clean the earth and its oceans. He will make them good places to live. He will make the water pure again. You will be able to swim in the oceans. They will be full of whales, dolphins, and fish again. You will be able to drink from the streams again.

All the land of the earth will be a paradise. Magnificent lions and leopards will roam the earth once more. And they will be even better than they are now. They won't hunt and kill animals anymore. They will be gentle and eat plants like cattle. All of the earth will be like the Garden of Eden.

"Then wolves will live in peace with lambs. And leopards will lie down to rest with goats. Calves, lions and young bulls will eat together. And a little child will lead them. Cows and bears will eat together in peace. Their young will lie down together. Lions will eat hay as oxen do. A baby will be able to play near a cobra's hole. A child will be able to put his hand into the nest of a poisonous snake. They will not hurt or destroy each other" (Isaiah 11:6–9 ICB).

How are some people wrecking the beautiful world we live in?

What will the earth be like when God makes it into a paradise?

88. WHY DOES THE BIBLE SAY MONEY IS EVIL?

\\\\\\\\\\\\\\\\\\\\\\\\\

Some people think the Bible says that money is evil—but the Bible doesn't say that. Money isn't good or evil. Some people use money to do good things. Other people use money to do evil things.

What the Bible says is this: "The love of money causes all kinds of evil" (1 Timothy 6:10 ICB). If you *love* money, it causes problems—lots of problems! For example, if you're eager to get money, you'll step on others to get it. If you're greedy for money, you'll cheat others. If you love money too much, you'll hang on to it selfishly. You won't share with needy people.

It all depends on your attitude toward money. The Bible says, "For the love of money is a source of all kinds of evil. Some have been so eager to have it that they have wandered away from the faith and have broken their hearts with many sorrows" (1 Timothy 6:10 GNT). How do selfish people wander away from the faith?

Well, Jesus said, "Freely you have received; freely give" (Matthew 10:8 NIV). Do you give unselfishly? Then you have true faith. And Jesus said, "If a person asks you for something, then give it to him. Don't refuse to give to a person who wants to borrow from you" (Matthew 5:42 ICB).

The apostle John warned, "If we are rich and

see others in need, yet close our hearts against them, how can we claim that we love God?" (1 John 3:17 GNT). If you don't help the poor and needy, you don't truly love God. If you don't love God, you've wandered from the faith.

Of course, you can't help *all* the needy people in the world. And you shouldn't give away all your money to the poor so that you have none left. It's not only good to be generous. It's also good to be wise. You have needs too.

Remember, money by itself is not evil. The Bible says, "It is not good to eat too much honey" (Proverbs 25:27 NIV). Does that mean honey is evil? No. Just *too much* honey is bad. The Bible also says, "If you find honey, eat just enough—too much of it, and you will vomit" (Proverbs 25:16 NIV). But honey is good, and you are supposed to eat it. "Eat honey, my son, for it is good" (Proverbs 24:13 NIV).

It's the same with money as with honey. You need money. Money can do a lot of good. But don't get greedy for too much of it.

Why isn't money evil?

If you're greedy for money, how do you wander from the faith?

89. WHY SHOULD I GO TO SCHOOL IF THE WORLD IS GOING TO END SOON?

\\\\\\\\\\\\\\\\\\\\\\\\

You might hear Christians say that the world will end soon. They say Jesus could return *any time*—even today. Some believers think He will wait a while before returning. But many people believe Jesus can't possibly wait even ten more years. And He will appear without any warning. Nothing special will be happening in the world. The day will start out like any other day. Then suddenly Jesus will appear. They think this because He said:

> "Stay alert! The coming of the Son of Man can be illustrated by the story of a man going on a long trip. When he left home, he gave each of his slaves instructions about the work they were to do, and he told the gatekeeper to watch for his return. You, too, must keep watch! For you don't know when the master of the household will return—in the evening, at midnight, before dawn, or at daybreak. Don't let him find you sleeping when he arrives without warning.... Watch for him!" (Mark 13:33–37 NLT)

But you may ask, "If the world is going to end so soon, why should I bother going to school? I'll barely graduate before Jesus returns. Why should I study for years to be a doctor or an engineer? Why should I get a job? Why should I save money for the future?"

But remember, Jesus also said, "He gave each of his slaves instructions about the work they were to do" (v. 34). Jesus has *work* for you to do on earth until He returns. So find out what it is, and study to learn how to do it. Then do it.

The apostle Paul started a church in Thessalonica, Greece. He told the Christians that Jesus would one day return. After Paul left, some of them began saying that the end of the world had come (see 2 Thessalonians 2:2). So certain believers began "living idle lives, refusing to work." Paul said, "We command such people. . .to settle down and work to earn their own living" (2 Thessalonians 3:11–12 NLT).

The truth is, we simply *don't know* when Jesus is going to return. He could return in just a few years. Or He could wait another hundred years. Whenever He returns, you don't want Him to find you doing nothing. Right? So study hard so you can get a good job when you finish school. Be all that God wants you to be!

Why shouldn't you sit around doing nothing till Jesus returns?

What work do you think Jesus has given you to do?

90. WHY DO PEOPLE NOT WANT US TO CELEBRATE CHRISTMAS?

\\\\\\\\\\\\\\\\\\\\\\\\\

For the first 450 years, many Americans thought of this as a Christian country. Schools had public prayers to God. Even students who didn't believe in God had to respect prayer time. Schools often prayed the Lord's Prayer every day. Then, some people argued that atheists and people of other religions were offended by these prayers. So in 1962, the Supreme Court said that public schools could no longer make students pray. Then, in 1963, it stopped Bible reading in schools.

Some courthouses in America had the Ten Commandments on their walls. Then some people fought to get the Ten Commandments taken down. They didn't stop there. Many cities in America put manger scenes in public places. They put Christmas trees in town squares. But people demanded that they remove them. They argued that those who weren't Christians were offended by these symbols.

Some people want all Americans to be "politically correct." A person who is politically correct never says anything that offends anyone else. But has this gone way too far? In the past, store clerks would say "Merry Christmas" to customers. Some people complained that the word "Christmas" offended them. So clerks were told to say, "Happy Holidays" instead.

Christians often tell others about Jesus in public parks. This angers some atheists, so they sometimes report the Christians to the police. At times, the police tell the Christians they have to leave the park. This isn't right. There are millions of Christians in America, and they have the freedom to live their faith. They have the right to share their faith with others. Don't let people take away these rights.

Christians understand about not offending people. They *get* that. The apostle Paul said, "We give no offense in anything, that our ministry may not be blamed" (2 Corinthians 6:3 NKJV). But many Christians feel like "political correctness" has gone way too far. If some people could do it, they would get rid of Christmas and Easter completely. They would like to stop Christians from witnessing about Jesus. But they can't do that. Christians have been standing up for their rights.

The good news is that Christians still have many freedoms in North America. You can have a manger scene in your home. You can have a Christmas tree in your house. You can go to church and worship God. You can tell others about Jesus. You have the right to do these things. Don't let anyone take them away from you.

Why were Bible reading and prayers taken out of public schools?

Why do some people not want to celebrate Christmas?

91. WHAT IS THE MARK OF THE BEAST?

\\\\\\\\\\\\\\\\\\\\\\

Many Christians think that we're living in the end times. They believe that a one-world government will soon rise and rule all nations. A man who has power from the devil will be the world ruler. He will pretend to be a good man, but he will actually be the Antichrist.

His helper, the False Prophet, will try to force everyone to worship the Antichrist. He will insist that they get a mark in their right hand or in their forehead. Without this mark, people won't be able to buy or sell anything. They will starve to death. And the Antichrist's soldiers will kill everyone who refuses to worship him.

The Bible says: "He required everyone—small and great, rich and poor, free and slave—to be given a mark on the right hand or on the forehead. And no one could buy or sell anything without that mark, which was either the name of the beast or the number representing his name. . . . His number is 666" (Revelation 13:16–18 NLT).

In Revelation 13, the Antichrist is called "the beast." That's why this mark is called the mark of the beast. Christians used to think that this mark was like a tattoo or a brand. Now many people think it will be a small computer chip. Scientists will put it under people's skin, and scanners will read it. If people want to buy food, they'll put their hand on a scanner. Then it will read the chip in their hand and take the money from their bank.

These days, people already put tiny computer chips in dogs' ears. If your dog is picked up by the pound, they can find out everything about him. They pass a handheld scanner over his ear, and it tells them his ID number. Then they can look up his owner's name and address on their computer.

Scientists have already started putting test chips in humans. Some people say this will make life easier. They won't have to carry identification. All their information is in the chip. But other people warn that this will take away their privacy. The government will know where they are at all times. They will know what people are doing. They will know everything about them.

The Bible warns that those who accept the mark of the beast, and worship the Antichrist, will go to hell. True Christians will run into the wilderness rather than receive the mark. But fortunately, it's not that time yet.

What do you think the mark of the beast is?

Why is it dangerous for rulers to know
   everything about you?

92. WHAT IS HELL, THE LAKE OF FIRE, LIKE?

\\\\\\\\\\\\\\\\\\\\\\\\\\\\\\

When we say "hell," we're talking about the lake of fire. We're not talking about the place of the dead where unsaved people go right after they die. That's bad enough. But the lake of fire is truly awful. We know that sinners will suffer there. But we don't know *exactly* what it's like. No one has gone there, then come back to talk about it.

The Bible says, "The devil, who deceived them, was cast into the lake of fire and brimstone where the beast and the false prophet *are*. And they will be tormented day and night forever and *ever*" (Revelation 20:10 NKJV). What is "the lake of fire and brimstone"? The NIV translates it as "the lake of burning sulfur." Have you ever smelled burning sulfur? It smells awful!

The Bible says the heavenly city is full of God's light (see Revelation 21:23). But the people who aren't allowed into heaven will be in "outer darkness" (Matthew 8:12 NLT).

Some people say God would never make people suffer in such a place. They say that when the Bible talks about "fire" it actually means people will be separated from God forever. Then they will wish they had chosen God. They will have a burning desire for Him. But it will be too late.

Other Christians think that evil people will suffer in hell. But they don't believe God would make them suffer *forever*. However, the Bible says they were "cast into the lake of fire and brimstone where. . .they will be tormented day and night forever and *ever*" (Revelation 20:10 NKJV). And Revelation 14:11 (GNT) says, "The smoke of the fire that torments them goes up forever and ever." That does sound like they will suffer for all eternity.

But other Christians believe that when people go into the lake of fire, they only suffer a short while. They simply burn up. Then they're gone. They think this because in Isaiah 34:9–10 (NLT) God describes Edom "filled with burning pitch, and. . .fire." It says, "This judgment on Edom will never end; the smoke of its burning will rise forever." Edom *was* destroyed, but that fire didn't actually burn forever. So they don't think the lake of fire will actually last forever either.

Whatever hell is like, it's not someplace you want to go. And the good news is you don't need to go there. You can be sure you'll go to heaven instead if you believe in Jesus.

Do you think unsaved people suffer in hell forever?

Is the lake of fire actual flames? Could the burning mean something else?

93. WHAT IS THE RAPTURE?

\\\\\\\\\\\\\\\\\\\\

You sometimes hear Christians talk about the Rapture. They say that it could happen today or tomorrow—or a few years from now. But what *is* the Rapture? It means "to be caught up" or "taken away." The apostle Paul wrote, "Then, together with them, we who are still alive and remain on the earth will be caught up in the clouds to meet the Lord in the air" (1 Thessalonians 4:17 NLT).

The Rapture happens when Jesus returns to earth to rescue Christians from this evil world. The Bible warns that things on earth will get worse and worse. A time of great trouble will come. It's called the seven years of Great Tribulation. Many Christians believe that Jesus will come just before it starts. He will take them to heaven. Other Christians believe that God will keep them on earth during the Tribulation. He will rescue them after it ends.

But no matter *when* they think Jesus will return, Christians believe He *will* return. He will come back in the clouds (Matthew 24:30–31; Revelation 1:7). The spirits of the Christians who have died will come with him. Their dead bodies will be changed into supernatural bodies. They will rise from earth into the sky. Then their spirits will enter their new bodies. After this, the Christians who are still living on earth will be changed. Their bodies will become powerful, eternal bodies.

Then they will rise into the sky to join Jesus and the other Christians.

Believers' dead bodies come back to life at the Resurrection. To "resurrect" means to rise from the dead. But they won't be old and weak anymore. Do you remember what Jesus' powerful, eternal body was like? This is how beautiful and majestic He looks *now*: "His head and his hair were white like wool, as white as snow. And his eyes were like flames of fire. His feet were like polished bronze refined in a furnace, and his voice thundered like mighty ocean waves. . . . And his face was like the sun in all its brilliance" (Revelation 1:14–16 NLT).

Jesus now has a glorious, eternal body. And Paul says "we eagerly wait for our Savior, the Lord Jesus Christ, to come from heaven. He will change our weak mortal bodies and make them like his own glorious body" (Philippians 3:20–21 GNT). Won't that be wonderful? We'll have eternal bodies as glorious as Jesus' body! The apostle John promised, "But we know that when Christ appears, we shall be like him" (1 John 3:2 GNT).

- -

What happens at the Rapture?

What will your eternal body be like?

94. WILL CHRISTIANS BE PUNISHED FOR BAD DEEDS?

\\\\\\\\\\\\\\\\\\\\\\\\\\

Many Christians think that even if you believe in Jesus, God will *still* punish you for your sins. Many Catholics believe that only very holy Christians go straight to heaven when they die. Most believers aren't pure enough. They're first sent to purgatory. There, fire burns away anything bad. Christians suffer in purgatory until all their sins are gone. Finally, they're pure enough to enter heaven.

How long do they think Christians suffer in purgatory? They believe people spend 1,000 to 2,000 years there. Some Catholics say you must suffer seven years for each sin. But if you repeat certain prayers over and over and over again, you can shorten your stay. For example, say you repeat the *Gloria Patris* prayer seven times a day, and say one *Ave Maria*. Then you will spend 100 days less in purgatory.

Many Catholics pray that God will let souls out of purgatory. Catholics used to believe that they could simply give money to the church, and God would forgive people's sins. But you can't pay money to forgive sins.

The Bible doesn't talk about purgatory. Instead, it says that all Christians are purified from their sins by the blood of Christ. "But if we confess our sins, he will forgive our sins. We can trust

God. He does what is right. He will make us clean from all the wrongs we have done" (1 John 1:9 ICB). Jesus makes you pure by His blood—not by sending you to purgatory to suffer in flames for thousands of years.

The Bible says, "For we must all stand before Christ to be judged. Each one will receive what he should get—good or bad—for the things he did when he lived in the earthly body" (2 Corinthians 5:10 ICB). Jesus will reward you for the good you have done. But all the useless deeds you have done will be burned up in an instant (see 1 Corinthians 3:11–15). They will be gone. You won't receive any reward for them.

Purgatory is judgment and suffering. Christians will *not* suffer God's punishment. "Anyone who believes in God's Son has eternal life. Anyone who doesn't obey the Son will never experience eternal life but remains under God's angry judgment" (John 3:36 NLT). "God chose to save us through our Lord Jesus Christ, not to pour out his anger on us" (1 Thessalonians 5:9 NLT).

Christians go straight to heaven when they die. Paul said, "I desire to depart and be with Christ" (Philippians 1:23 NIV).

Do you believe Christians suffer in fire for 2,000 years after they die?

Why do you believe that God saves you and takes you to heaven?

95. WHERE IS HEAVEN?

\\\\\\\\\\\\\\\\\\\\\\\

Many people think heaven is in the clouds. They get this idea from reading about Jesus' return to earth. "They will see the Son of Man coming on the clouds of heaven" (Matthew 24:30 NLT). "After that. . .We will be taken up in the clouds to meet the Lord in the air. And we will be with the Lord forever" (1 Thessalonians 4:17 ICB).

When Jesus returns, He will appear in the sky where everyone can see Him. Then you shall be caught up to meet Him in the clouds. But you don't stay there. That's not heaven. That's just where you meet Jesus. Once you join Him *then* Jesus takes you to heaven. If you take a bus to school, you know what this is like. The bus stop isn't school. You wait at the stop for the bus, and when it comes, you ride to school. But going to heaven is much, much better than going to school.

If heaven isn't in the sky, where *is* it? Is it in outer space among the stars? Some people think so. A Bible man named Job said, "God is in the highest part of heaven. See how high the highest stars are!" (Job 22:12 ICB).

King Solomon explained, however, that not even the highest heaven could hold God. Solomon built a temple for God. A lot of Israelites thought that the Lord would come down to live there. But Solomon knew that God was too big to fit inside the temple. Solomon said, "Not even the highest of heavens can hold God" (2 Chronicles 2:6 ICB). God is everywhere at once and fills up our universe (Psalm 139:5–10).

If God is too big to fit inside our universe, where *else* does He live? He also lives *outside* the universe in "eternity" (Isaiah 57:15 NKJV). He lives in the spiritual dimension. A dimension is like another world right beside this world, only you can't see it. Heaven is in another dimension.

Sometimes there's an opening between the two dimensions. In the story, *The Lion, The Witch, and The Wardrobe*, four children were living in an old house in England. But when they walked through a wardrobe (closet), they came out the other side into a world called Narnia. Now, Narnia is only a made-up story, but you get the idea. It was right beside our world, but was outside it. That's what the heavenly dimension is like.

God is everywhere at once and fills up our universe. Can you explain this?

Where do you think heaven is? Why do you think that?

96. WHAT IS HEAVEN LIKE?

\\\\\\\\\\\\\\\\\\\\\\\\\\

The Bible says that heaven is a huge city called New Jerusalem, and it shines with the glory of God. It's made out of gold like transparent glass, and has streets of pure gold too. It has twelve gates made of pearl. The River of Life flows through the city, and Trees of Life grow along the river. It has fountains of living water.

Are all these things real? Yes! They're real. We'll have eternal bodies, and we'll need eternal homes to live in. We'll need solid floors and streets to walk on. If this wasn't so, Jesus would have said so. He said, "There are many rooms in my Father's house. I would not tell you this if it were not true. I am going there to prepare a place for you" (John 14:2 ICB). You can be sure that the place Jesus has prepared for you is real. And it's more fantastic than anything you can imagine.

The Bible says, "The street of the city was pure gold, like transparent glass" (Revelation 21:21 NKJV). In fact, the entire city is made of the same amazing gold. "The city itself was made of pure gold, as clear as glass" (Revelation 21:18 GNT). Is God's city and its streets actually made of transparent gold? Well, since God Himself lives there, of course everything is glorious and fantastic! It makes earthly gold and jewels seem like cheap imitations.

There's another reason that the buildings and

the streets are see-through. John wrote: "The city does not need the sun or moon to shine on it. God's glory is its light, and the Lamb is its lamp" (Revelation 21:23 NIV). The glory of God and Jesus fills the city. All of New Jerusalem is lit up with the light of God. It shines through every wall and street and building.

Jesus made a promise about your home in heaven: "In My Father's house are many mansions" (John 14:2 NKJV). Many believers dream of their own gorgeous palace. But another Bible translation says it this way: "There are many rooms in my Father's house" (John 14:2 ICB). So we might all be living in one huge palace that's as big as the whole city. One thing we know: Jesus is preparing a wonderful home in eternity.

Another name for heaven is Paradise. A "paradise" is a royal park full of lovely flower gardens, fruit trees, shady walking paths, fish ponds, streams, fountains, songbirds, butterflies, peacocks, graceful deer, magnificent horses, and tame lions and tigers.

Of all the things in heaven, what do you look forward to the most?

Can you imagine a see-through gold city glowing with God's light?

97. WILL WE PLAY HARPS AND PRAISE GOD ALL THE TIME IN HEAVEN?

\\\\\\\\\\\\\\\\\\\\\\\\\\\

Many people have silly ideas about heaven. They think that heaven is nothing but fluffy, white clouds. They think that people will have big, white wings and will fly up and sit on the clouds. They'll sit there and spend all their time playing harps and singing hymns. You probably hope that this is just someone's imagination. It's not something you'd enjoy doing forever and ever. Yes, it's just people's guesses.

Mind you, the Bible talks about *some* believers playing harps in heaven. "They were standing. . . holding harps that God had given them and singing. . .the song of the Lamb: 'Lord God Almighty, how great and wonderful are your deeds! King of the nations, how right and true are your ways!'" (Revelation 15:2–3 GNT).

And the Bible *does* talk about praising God with harp music. "Sing praises to the LORD! Play music on the harps!" (Psalm 98:5 GNT). But most people have no idea how to play a harp. So it would sound awful if millions of these people were trying to play a harp at once.

The apostle John wrote, "I looked, and there was an enormous crowd—no one could count all the people! They were from every race, tribe, nation, and language, and they stood in front of the throne and of the Lamb, dressed in white robes and holding palm branches in their hands. They called out in a loud voice: 'Salvation comes from our God, who sits on the throne, and from the Lamb!' All the angels stood around the throne, the elders, and the four living creatures. Then they threw themselves face downward in front of the throne and worshiped God" (Revelation 7:9–12 GNT).

After reading that, some people think that that's *all* that people in heaven *ever* do—stand around God's throne all the time, praising Him. They get that idea because they don't read their Bibles very carefully.

These gatherings around God's throne are probably on special occasions. People won't gather in huge crowds like that all the time. The heavenly Jerusalem is a very big place. It's full of many other interesting, exciting, and fun activities. Besides, when you see God face-to-face in heaven, you won't find it boring to praise Him. God is incredibly beautiful. Worshipping Him will give you great happiness. You'll probably have a hard time pulling your eyes away from Him.

If God is so beautiful and awesome, what will it be like to see Him?

Will harps be the *only* musical instruments in heaven? Why do you think that?

98. WILL MY PET BE IN HEAVEN?

\\\\\\\\\\\\\\\\\\\\\\\\\\

Heaven is a place where you'll be perfectly happy forever. For many people, something would be missing if their pet wasn't there. So most likely, yes, your favorite pets will be in heaven. The famous preacher, Billy Graham, said, "God will prepare everything for our perfect happiness in heaven, and if it takes my dog being there, I believe he'll be there."

When Jesus rules the earth, it will be turned into a paradise (see Isaiah 11:1–9). There will be animals there such as wolves, bears, leopards, lions, sheep and lambs, goats and kids, cattle and calves. . .and even snakes. After Jesus rules this planet for a thousand years, God will create a new earth. The heavenly city will be on earth then (see Revelation 21:1–3). And there will still be animals around!

God told the prophet Isaiah, "Look! I am creating new heavens and a new earth. . . . The wolf and the lamb will feed together. The lion will eat hay like a cow. But the snakes will eat dust. In those days no one will be hurt or destroyed on my holy mountain" (Isaiah 65:17, 25 NLT).

Isaiah didn't mention dogs, but if even *wolves* are there, you can be sure that dogs will be too. Many people like wandering with their dog along shady paths through a park. And heaven is the perfect paradise. So romping with your beloved dog across green lawns, past trees and fountains, will be truly heavenly. And if even *lions* are in heaven, pet cats will be there too. There will be all kinds of animals in heaven.

Also, good news for horse lovers: the Bible says that there are large herds of horses in heaven (Revelation 19:11, 14). So you will be able to enjoy riding a horse through huge fields of flowers. And even if you don't have a pet you'd like to see in heaven, there will still be lots of animals there. You will be able to pet tame lions and play-wrestle with tigers. You will be able to fly with flocks of snow-white swans. You will be able to swim with colorful tropical fish. You will be able to ride through the water on the backs of giant sea turtles.

There will probably even be a dinosaur area of heaven—like an enormous zoo. You will be able to get real close to these awesome monsters. After all, God created dinosaurs also, and they're some of His most amazing creatures.

Which of your pets do you look forward to seeing in heaven?

What kinds of new animals do you want to play with in heaven?

99. WHAT WILL PEOPLE DO IN HEAVEN?

\\\\\\\\\\\\\\\\\\\\\\\\\

What will you do in heaven? Well, what do you enjoy doing on earth now? You probably like watching movies, playing games, exploring, eating yummy food, and learning interesting things. You'll very likely do all that and more in heaven! You didn't think there were movies and fun things to do in heaven? You'll probably be able to watch movies of all the adventures of the Bible heroes.

One of the best things about heaven is that you'll be together again with your loved ones. You're sad when they die. But in heaven, you'll never have to say "goodbye" again. Imagine walking through paradise with your great-great-grandfather! Think of all the stories he could tell you about your family.

There will be all kinds of delicious food to eat in heaven. Jesus said, "I assure you that many will come from the east and the west and sit down with Abraham, Isaac, and Jacob at the feast in the Kingdom of heaven" (Matthew 8:11 GNT). If you believe in Jesus, you're invited to this banquet! What food will you feast on? Jesus promises, "I will give the hidden manna to everyone who wins the victory" (Revelation 2:17 ICB). Manna is heavenly food that tastes like wafers and honey. God also promises that you'll eat the fruit of the Tree of Life (Revelation 22:2).

You'll learn all kinds of new things too. There is so, so much that you don't know, and you'll never stop learning in heaven. You won't have to sit in school and study boring things. You'll study things that you're interested in and enjoy learning about. You'll be doing lots of exciting jobs that you never did before. So you will need to learn how to do them.

You'll be able to ask the great men and women of God questions, and finally get answers. Angels will be your teachers too. Angels have been asking questions a long time. They've learned a lot! That's why, all through the Bible, angels have been explaining things to people.

And you will rule over the earth. Some Christians "will rule as kings forever and ever" (Revelation 22:5 GNT). There will be nations and cities and towns and villages all over the earth. So, God's Kingdom will need kings and queens to rule over nations. It will need governors to rule provinces and states. It will need mayors to govern cities and towns and villages. And it will need wise men and women to advise the rulers.

What kinds of things would you like to do in heaven?

Who are you looking forward to meeting in heaven?

100. WHAT WILL I DO FOR ALL ETERNITY?

\\\\\\\\\\\\\\\\\\\\\\

What will you do after you do everything you could imagine doing on this earth? What will you do after you've explored every corner of the heavenly city? You'll probably be able to explore other planets. After you've learned everything about the heavenly city and the earth, you can visit millions of amazing new worlds.

Recently, scientists discovered that our sun is not the only star with planets. They've found hundreds of planets orbiting nearby stars. Scientists think our galaxy—the Milky Way galaxy—has about 50 billion planets. And 500 million of them are about the size of earth. And they're "Goldilocks planets." That means they're not too close to their star so they're burning. And they're not too far from their star so they're frozen. They're "just right," like in the story *Goldilocks and the Three Bears*.

Think of it! About 500 million planets (just in the Milky Way galaxy) may be able to support life. Is Earth really the only world with life? Probably not. And when you finally, finally explore all 500 million of those planets, you've *just begun*! Because there are about 170 billion galaxies in the universe. You'll never, ever run out of things to do and see.

The Bible says, "[God] stretches out the heavens like a curtain, and spreads them out like a tent to dwell in" (Isaiah 40:22 NKJV). God probably created planets like earth to live on. "The Lord created the heavens. He is the God who formed the earth. . . . But he did not want it to be empty. He wanted life to be on the earth." (Isaiah 45:18 ICB).

There will be desert planets. There will be jungle planets. There will be water planets. And many of them may have strange and beautiful plants and colorful, amazing animals on them. Now, we don't know for sure if there's life on other worlds. But if there is, remember that it was God (through Jesus) who created it. "All things were made through Him, and without Him nothing was made that was made" (John 1:3 NKJV).

Some people wonder if there's intelligent life on alien planets. That's really guessing! The Bible doesn't tell us, so we simply don't know. But we *do* know that every intelligent being in the universe will one day worship Jesus. "At the name of Jesus every knee should bow, of those in heaven, and of those on earth. . .and *that* every tongue should confess that Jesus Christ *is* Lord" (Philippians 2:10–11 NKJV).

What kind of alien world would you like to explore most of all?

If there is life on other planets, who created it?

101. WHY CAN'T I GO TO HEAVEN NOW?

\\\\\\\\\\\\\\\\\\\\\\\\\

When you read about how wonderful it is in the heavenly city, you may want to go there now. People there are happy. But you may be sad now. Maybe you're sick or going through a difficult time. Maybe a loved one has died, and you want to be with them. Or you might have problems now, and problems make you sad. So you may wonder why you should stay on earth. Wouldn't it be easier and better to go to heaven?

It might be *easier*, but it might not be better. It's probably not what God wants. Why is that? Because you still have a job to do on earth. God wants you to live your life here, following Jesus' teachings. You must obey Him day after day— even in difficult days. Then, when *God* decides it's time to take you to heaven, He will take you.

God doesn't usually give you a choice about when you go. He did give the apostle Paul a choice. But Paul was an old man, and he had been whipped and beaten and stoned many times. He was just about worn out. He was ready for heaven. But he *still* didn't know what to choose.

Paul wrote: "For to me, living means living for Christ, and dying is even better. But if I live, I can do more fruitful work for Christ. So I really don't know which is better. I'm torn between two desires: I long to go and be with Christ, which would be far better for me. But for your sakes, it is better that I continue to live. Knowing this, I am convinced that I will remain alive so I can continue to help all of you" (Philippians 1:21–25 NLT).

It was better for *Paul* that he went to heaven. But it was better for *others* that he stayed on earth and helped them. So he decided he'd stay. Christians can't always decide to do what is easiest for them. They must think about other people. You can't go to heaven just because life is difficult.

You may ask, "But can't I just visit heaven for a short while, then come back?" If it's God's will, you can do that. Paul did. He went up to paradise (see 2 Corinthians 12:2–4). And the apostle John did. He visited God's throne in heaven (see Revelation 4:1–2). But remember, very few people are allowed to visit heaven.

Why is it usually better for people not to go to heaven right away?

When will God take you to heaven?

ABOUT THE AUTHOR

Ed Strauss is a freelance writer living in British Columbia, Canada. He has authored or coauthored more than fifty books for children, tweens, and adults. Ed has a passion for Biblical apologetics and besides writing for Barbour, has been published by Zondervan, Tyndale, Moody, and Focus on the Family.

ARE YOUR CHILDREN READY FOR THEIR FIRST DEVOTIONAL?

It All Matters to Jesus Devotional for Boys

Ever wonder if Jesus really cares about your new bike, your favorite app, or how you treat your little sister? Each of the 40 brief devotional chapters in *It All Matters to Jesus* offers reassurance that He does care whether or not you told a "little white lie" at school...how you treat Mom and Dad...how you spend your free time...your daily struggles and cares... He cares about every little—and BIG—thing. Find the heavenly Father in life's daily details and come to know just how much He cares for you!

Paperback / 978-1-63058-921-9 / $5.99

It All Matters to Jesus Devotional for Girls

Each of the 40 devotional chapters offers girls reassurance that it all really does matters to Jesus! How girls treat their siblings...what they write about in their journals...how they treat Mom and Dad...how they spend their free time—painting, drawing, dancing, spending time in God's Word—their daily struggles and cares... He cares about every little—and BIG—thing.

Paperback / 978-1-63058-933-2 / $5.99